DISCOVER
Y⊕URSELF!
The Epic Soul Search To Uncover Who You Really Are

A Course In Personal Development

Textbook Written By: Carolyn Waldbueser

Graphic Design and Art Layout: April Waldbueser

Published by Catwalk Productions 2015. ©

Photo images © Shutterstock.com
All artwork © April Waldbueser

ISBN: 978-0-9970794-0-1

Printed and bound in the United States of America

TABLE OF CONTENTS:

SECTION 1: DISCOVER YOUR DESIRE TO CHANGE

SECTION 2: DISCOVER YOUR COURAGE TO DREAM

SECTION 3: DISCOVER YOUR PASSION TO CREATE

ABOUT THE

CAROLYN WALDBUESER

has been a leader in the fashion industry for over 30 years. She is the director of Miami Fashion Board, producing the nation's largest network of runway stage events. She is also the CEO of Catwalk Productions which publishes Pose Magazine.

For over three decades, Carolyn has mentored models who have appeared on the covers of

VOGUE, MARIE CLAIRE, GLAMOUR, & SHAPE MAGAZINE.

She has developed new faces who have appeared in ads for top clients such as :

CALVIN KLEIN, HOLLISTER, ESTÉE LAUDER, KOHLS, TARGET, CLAIRE'S, AND MACY'S.

Born in 1954 in Springvale, Georgia, Carolyn is a Cum Laude graduate of the University of Georgia. Her books and workshops have helped thousands of people learn the secrets to success and achieve their goals beyond their wildest dreams.

Carolyn and her husband, Bill, have been married for 38 years. Their proudest achievements are their six children and nine grandchildren.

To contact Carolyn's team email: Carolyn@CatwalkStageProductions.com

AUTHOR

A note FROM The Author

Do you have the courage to take your first step toward a new dream?

I have witnessed ordinary people attain extra ordinary dreams. I have observed the rise and fall of many careers and relationships. I have seen the thrill of victory and the agony of defeat.

DISCOVER YOU is a step by step journey that will lead you toward truth and away from illusions. It is a path that will take you through the looking glass to achieve your greatest potential. My wish is that this book will inspire you to look into the mirror and discover your true reflection. My hope is that you will learn how to look past your physical image and gaze into your soul. My prayer is that you will uncover the part of you that is beyond what your eyes can see. Discovering your real identity will change your life forever. Unleashing who you really are will give you the power to redefine your destiny. Uncovering your authentic self will give you the passion to dream, and the power to win.

Do you believe in fate? Do you believe in synchronicity and coincidences? Do you believe that you are reading this book for a reason? The reason is because this is your time. The reason is because this is the adventure that you have been waiting to begin. The part of you that you have kept hidden for too long is ready to emerge. Get ready... get set... To DISCOVER YOURSELF!

bitterness
authentic quirky
creative
depressed
jealous
positive stressed
disgust
unique
unforgettable betrayal
beautiful insecure
grumpy
nice
charming
talented
selfish
energetic conflict
confident
boredom
paranoid
love
anger kind
charismatic
anxiety
grateful fabulous
cute success
sadness
rage
obssesive
lonely responsible
fear
addiction
passion foolish
adorable lazy
regret ambitious

sweet
cold
ashamed
otherwise
hate
guilt
liar
wise
sexy
interesting
negative

shy
amazing
gifted

GET REAL!

☐ **STEP 1**

Breast Implants! Plastic Surgery! Botox! Hair Extensions! Capped Teeth! False Eyelashes! Facelifts! Acrylic Nails! Spray Tans! Sadly, we live in a world of artificial beauty. This book is an epic soul search to uncover your real identity. Technology can actually now produce artificial intelligence. The cosmetic industry is now so advanced, that we can now literally cover any flaw and conceal any imperfection. We can significantly change the shape of our nose, or remove fat cells from our waistline. We eat hybrid food and drink Coke, "the real thing." But, is it really real? What is REAL anymore? As we stand posed in front of the camera, ready for our close up, there's still something missing... What is it that's not quite right? What's wrong with the picture? Oh yeah, it's the one thing that cannot be artificial. It's the only thing that you can't cover up or conceal... our FAKE SMILE! Lipstick can't correct it. Botox can't help! A real smile comes from the beauty that is inside of you. A natural smile is created by discovering the you that is beyond what you see in the mirror.

If Charlie Sheen is WINNING, then who is losing?

Behind closed doors, we are all searching for real happiness. Behind the masks that we wear in public, we are uncomfortable with who we see in the mirror. Behind your fear... beyond your insecurities, there is a part of you on the inside that has been waiting for you... waiting for this moment... waiting for you to unplug from technology and be silent... waiting for you to escape from the crowds to be alone in SOLITUDE... waiting for you to stop being so busy to be STILL for long enough to discover who you really are. The Best Thing About Me Is: _____

"Today you are you. That is truer than true.
There is no one alive, who is youer than you!
- The Cat In The Hat

Leave the
Masquerade
Charade!

One day a year on Halloween, it's OK to dress up and be someone else. Put on a mask or a costume and pretend to be a princess or a pirate. You can portray a super hero or a hobo... it's what you do on Halloween. Unfortunately, many people wear their disguises all year long. Pretending to be someone that you're not is the ultimate definition of a hypocrite. Are you a chameleon that changes colors depending on the group that you are with? Do you even remember what your true colors really are?

Have you stayed too long at the masquerade ball? Like Cinderella, it is almost midnight and it is time to reveal your true identity. When the things that you do, do not follow your heart... and the things that you say, do not truly express who you are... you are risking being exposed as a phony. When you change your values and your standards, as often as you change your clothes, it might be time to run away from the masquerade ball.

To save your true authentic self, you need to run as fast as you can. It's OK if you drop your slipper. Go ahead and drop all of your fake attachments. Leave behind the artificial you that you pretend to be. Is your fancy car just a pumpkin pretending to be a carriage? Get rid of it! Are your friends really rats that are pretending to be coachmen? Say good bye, and good riddance.

☐ STEP 2

Deep inside all of us, there is a Fairy Godmother with a magic wand! Bippoty... Boppity.. Boo! Like Cinderella, have the courage to step outside of the shadows and reveal who you really are. Don't be ashamed or afraid. If you stop pretending... if you take off your mask... if you expose the real you... you just might find your Prince Charming. You just might find yourself living

happily ever after!

> ## " I am beautiful.
> ## No matter what they say.
> ## Words can't
> ## bring me down. "
> – Christina Aguilera

7

I Am Amazing Because: _____ **8**

HAVE AN IDENTITY

☐ STEP 3

Crisis

What would a man be if he took away his connection to his own economic, political or religious affiliations? Who would Donald Trump be if suddenly he found himself penniless? Would he lose his self confidence? Who would Tyra Banks be if she gained 50 pounds unexpectedly? Would she still feel beautiful? Are any of your labels who you really are? Most labels are temporary. They can change from day to day. If you are a girlfriend, what happens if your boyfriend breaks up with you? Who are you then? What happens to a cheerleader's facebook page when the last game is over, and she hangs up her pom-poms forever? Does she have to find a new hashtag? If a nerd takes off his glasses and his braces, and discovers that his label changes to a stud, is he a handsome nerd? Or a nerdy stud? If a rich man loses all of his money in the stock market, is he a poor rich man? If a poor man wins the lottery, is he a rich poor man? What happens to a woman's self esteem, when her husband leaves her, and she finds herself all alone? How does her identity evolve as her label changes from wife to ex-wife?

Circle the labels that you wear:
Hello, let me introduce myself. I am a...

Wife	Cheerleader	Student	Athlete	Beauty
Painter	Blogger	Rapper	Teacher	American
Catholic	Jogger	Soldier	Teenager	Christian
Rock Star	Dancer	Stud	Sr. Citizen	Grandchild
Cousin	Smoker	Mother	Brother	Football Fan
Model	Nerd	Player	Musician	Criminal
Girlfriend	Son	Swimmer	Singer	Comedian

Now add additional temporary labels that describe who you are:

_____   _____   _____

OK, now it's confusing. Am I just a bunch of words that describe activities that I do? Who does the younger athlete become, when they are older and can no longer play the game? Do they label themselves a former athlete? What about children who suddenly become stepchildren? Does changing a label suddenly change who you are?

Are you ready for the adventure of a lifetime? For once, quit listening to the noises all around you. Stop looking for your identity from labels that come and go. As you read this book, you will notice that you will begin to hear the voice that is inside of you. You will sense a calling to be still, and listen to your inner wisdom. You may have vivid dreams that keep your attention after you wake up. This book will open your ears, to the voice of your authentic self. That little voice that whispers in your ear is your own conscious. Are you ready to listen? Are you tired of the constant chatter of the world? Shhh! Listen carefully....

WHO AM I?

"After a while, *you learn* how to forget the names people call you... and just be **be who you are.**"
- Shrek

Grow ROOTS

☐ **STEP 4**

There are two different types of people. People who try... and people who criticize people who try. The ones who try have the courage to walk down life's path. The other group prefers to stand on the side of the path and throw stones at the tryers that walk by.

At a football game, about 50,000 people watch from the side lines, as about 50 people actually play the game. Sometimes they cheer. Sometimes they boo. Champion athletes do not listen to the noise from the crowd. They are on their own path of life, playing to win. The critics on the side are also on their own path, satisfied not to play, but just to watch someone else win.

The group of people that have the courage to walk down the path are the ones that pull strength and courage from deep down inside of them. There is a limitless source of supply, hidden deep within the well of their own soul. Shallow people on the sidelines of life are too busy criticizing others or throwing stones to discover their own deep well! The deeper you have dug down into your soul, the higher you can climb in life.

> ## "The moment you doubt whether you can fly,
> ### you cease the ability to do it."
> — Peter Pan

The height of a tree is directly related to the depths of its roots. A tree with lofty branches, but shallow roots, will certainly blow over in a storm. People who want to reach great heights in life without developing deep inner strength, will also get blown away with the winds of everyday adversities. Nothing in life is free. Depth is the price that must be paid to reach the heights.

In Japan, the bonsai tree's roots are bound and constricted continuously. When the roots are inhibited from growth, the tree's ability to grow is also stifled. The bound roots of the bonsai caused the stunted growth of the tree. Therefore, a 50 year old tree that should be 30 feet tall is reduced to a 1 foot miniature version of itself. Its limbs never bare fruit. It is not tall enough to provide shade. It serves no purpose, other than to be something to look at. It Is a sad life for a tree... that doesn't grow its roots, down deep into the **soil**. It is a sad life for us, if we don't grow our roots down deep into our own **soul**.

If you are in the group of people that walk down the path of life, STAND TALL! Become like the palm tree that can bend in the wind of a hurricane... Become like the redwood tree that soars to unimaginable heights. Become like the fruit trees, who gives of themselves to feed the whole world! Rise above "the bonsai people" on the sidelines, throwing stones at your knees.

I Am A Talented: _____

12

Brainwash

Yourself!

Spinach... Yum! I love it. **Spinach.**.. Yuck! I hate it. Spinach is neither good nor bad. Spinach is just spinach. It's the mind's conditioning that makes spinach so tasty or so nasty. If your mother liked spinach, then you probably like spinach. Do mothers brainwash their children? Absolutely! Indian mothers teach their children to love Indian food. Cuban mothers teach their children to love Cuban food. GET USED TO IT... your family brainwashes you. In Iran, a women is labeled as a harlot, if she does not cover her head. In contrast, Miss America performs in the bathing suit competition and wins a crown. GET OVER IT... Your culture brainwashes you.

Jews believe pork is unclean and unhealthy. Baptist believe bacon is literally heaven on earth. GET REAL... Your religion also brainwashes you.

Everyone, yes everyone, is brainwashed. The brain washing just depends on who you are listening to. Are you embarrassed at the thought, that great truths that you took for granted, were actually just made up by someone else's opinion of that truth?

What else do you believe because of tradition, rather than because of fact? What is something that you have always forced yourself to believe, when deep down in your gut, you have always felt something was wrong... something was missing? Do you vegetate in front of the television allowing the media to hypnotize you? Do you vote for someone just because they belong to your political party? The solution is, of course, to **brainwash yourself**. Don't just believe everything that you're taught. Study... research... and read for yourself. Question dogma and doctrine that don't make sense to you. Search for the real truth. Become a constant seeker. Make your own decision about who God is to you. Don't follow the crowds. Instead, trust your own instincts and intuition. Think for yourself. Make up your own mind... Do you like **spinach** or not?

> **"To find yourself... think for yourself."**
> -Socrates

I Will Make Up My Mind To: _____

☐ STEP 6 Take A

MAGIC CARPET

To say the word **yes** is to accept life in its total package. Say **yes** to the morning, because it brings back the light. Also, say **yes** to the evening, because it provides the time to rest. Say yes to the sunshine, because it causes the plants to grow. Also, say **yes** to the storm, because it too, causes the plants to grow. Easy, right? No problem, right? Well, try this one. Say **yes** to happiness, because it feels good. Also say **yes** to sadness, because.... WHAT?.... WAIT A MINUTE! Is that a typo mistake? Certainly you say **no** to sadness, don't you?

Acceptance of what is... is the secret key to bliss. Riding the storm of circumstances with no resistance, is the magic carpet ride of life. The next time you find yourself in a situation that you cannot change, don't fret, say **yes**! The next time you discover that you are surrounded by situations that will not go away, don't panic, say **yes**! **No** creates negative emotions that will only create unhappiness and frustration.

Instead, speak the magic word of the universe. **Yes** says to the universe "I trust you". **No** says to the universe "I do not trust you". **Yes,** is the abracadabra of the ages. Even if you are afraid, say **yes**! Even if you don't understand, say **yes**! **Yes** is your ticket to ride the magic carpet. Yes is your boarding pass to contentment and happiness. Accept what is. Don't resist what you cannot change. **Yes** allows you to catch your breath. **Yes** is letting go of the controls.

The other choice is to say **no**. Saying **no** to something you cannot change is to make yourself miserable. Not accepting the cards that life has dealt you is to live a life in denial and bitterness. The word **no**, will not summon the magic carpet ride. The word no leaves you abandoned and alone, on the road to nowhere. Change your **no** to **yes**.

Yes takes you on a mysterious magical journey to somewhere else. **Yes** alone rides the magic carpet that lifts you above your circumstances.

And one day, you will reach your final destination. For all of us, our goodbye to earth is not if, but when. We all end the journey of life, at the gate to eternity. How will you cross over? Will you go kicking and screaming, saying **no!** The final stop on the magical carpet ride of **yes** is to be transported from mortal to immortal... from the finite to infinity... from life to afterlife... from **no** to **yes**.

I Will Say Yes To: _____

"To infinity and beyond"
- Buzz Lightyear from Toy Story

Be Your Own HERO!

> ## "HEROES are made by the path that they choose, NOT BY THE POWER that they possess." -Iron Man

Who you are is not based on your outside appearance. A beauty queen can be pretty today and scarred tomorrow. A model can be skinny today and fat in 5 years. **Who you are** is not based on what you do. Jobs come and go. Relationships change and families evolve. Don't let your identity ride the roller coasters of life's ups and downs. Don't align your self image with the twists and turns of society. Be careful what you tattoo on your body. Things always change.

So then, apart from all the labels, all the jobs, all the relationships, who the heck are you? Learning who you are will take time. In the same way that oil lies deep beneath the surface, **the valuable you is hidden deep beneath all of your shallow labels.** Search for your true identity. Dig deeper until you discover something more. Something invisible will become visible. There is more to you than you have ever imagined. Under your shallow personality and nerdy glasses... just like Clark Kent, there is a Superman hidden beneath the surface. Even if you are a coward on the outside, there is a real hero hidden inside of all of us.

Sadly, many celebrities and athletes spiral down quickly when their 15 minutes of fame is over and the label is gone. When the ego is based on the praise of others, it collapses when the praise stops. When the personality is based on the label that is being worn, it disintegrates when the label changes. Champions become former champions. Wives become ex-wives. Take off all of your current labels... Who are you now?

Where does your identity come from? From your looks? From your relationships? From your social status? There is a part of you that has been waiting for you... waiting for this moment... waiting for the temporary mortal part of you to be introduced to the eternal divine part of you. Look behind your low self esteem. Look behind your prideful ego. **There, you will uncover the real you, disconnected from all of the labels.** The you that has been waiting patiently since you were born is ready to be revealed. Your real authentic self has been hidden, ignored, and tucked away long enough.

Buddha sat under a tree for years until he found his true identity. Moses went to the wilderness for forty years to discover the leader that was inside of him. Jesus went to the desert to face his shadow. Meditation and prayer are the digging tools. Silence, solitude, and stillness must become your new companions.

Clark Kent never changed identities in the public view. Even Superman had to go inside of the privacy of a telephone booth to take off his superficial self and uncover the hero inside of him.

My Hero Is: _____

19

SHED YOUR SKIN

Times, they are a changing.... The seasons change every year. Summer changes into Fall, and Winter changes into Spring. Life continually evolves and transforms into something new... something better. To be one with the universe; we too, must evolve day by day... season by season. We must become wiser as we get older. We must become the metamorphoses of the caterpillar to the butterfly. Change is an instinct.

On the surface, we change our hairstyle frequently. We change our wardrobe season to season. Out with the old and in with the new. Below the surface, underneath our shallow egos, deep within our souls, there is also a hunger for change.

BECOME LIKE A SNAKE that sheds its skin, when it has outgrown its size and has no further use for it. Take off the old man and put on the new. Throw away negative emotions, such as anger and bitterness, and replace them with kindness and patience. Step by step, little by little... rebuild your attitude... reinvent your personality... and reshape your destiny. Find a quiet place where you can be still and contemplate the necessary changes. Eventually, you will discover a place of deep serenity within yourself, the very center of your being.

The most important part of your skin to shed is the layer of fear. Fear of rejection and fear of failure keep most people locked inside of themselves, afraid to come out and become someone new. What will people think? What if I fail? The burden of carrying around the old weight of the dead useless part of you is like a snake that can't shed its skin. It's time to break free. It's time to unlock the door to your future.

NOW IS THE TIME TO COME OUT OF YOUR SHELL... TODAY IS THE DEBUT OF YOUR NEW IDENTITY.

"I meditate and pray everyday. I am still a work in progress."
-Halle Berry

I Will Change: _____

SHED Your Image

The following people shed their skin, changed their name, and found a new identity.

I AM / I WAS

Reginald Dwight	Elton John
Norma Jean Baker	Marilyn Monroe
Sidartha	Buddha
Simon	Peter
Demetria Guynes	Demi Moore
Margaret Hyra	Meg Ryan
Carlos Estevez	Charlie Sheen
Chaim Witz	Gene Simmons
Abram	Abraham
Richard Starsky	Ringo Starr
Annie Mae Bullock	Tina Turner
Steve Hardaway	Stevie Wonder
Saul	Paul
Marian Morrison	John Wayne
Francis Gumona	Judy Garland
Allan Konignberg	Woody Allen
Destiny Hope Cyrus	Miley Rae Cyrus
Thomas Mapother	Tom Cruise
Paul Hawson	Bono
Nick Coppola	Nicholas Cage
Jacob	Israel
Vincent Furnier	Alice Cooper
Henry Deutchendorf	John Denver
Caryn Johnson	Whoopi Goldberg
Archibold Leach	Cary Grant
Carlos Ray	Chuck Norris
Jean Molinsky	Joan Rivers

Imagine and pretend. Give yourself a brand new name that expresses your authentic self:

_____.

"I just want to be *wonderful!*"

-Marilyn Monroe

SQUEEZE
The Juice Out Of Life

☐ **STEP 10** — "When life gets you down , do you wanna know what you've gotta do? **Just keep swimming!**" – Finding Nemo

The juice of the fruit is like the fragrance of the flower. The juice is the sweet stuff. It is the most flavorful part of the whole fruit. Orange juice, apple juice, grape juice... all make your mouth water, thinking about their cool refreshing flavor. Tart or tangy... sweet or sour... it doesn't matter the type of fruit, the nectar of all of them is irresistible.

The elixir of life is similar to the juice of fruit. Even if life's juices are sour like a lemon; cheer up, you can always make lemonade. When you are squeezed in life, what emotions come out? If someone hurts your feelings, do you pour out pungent responses? If someone rejects you, do you squirt out bitterness? Squeezing is the pressure that forces a fruit to release its juice. We are all fruit on the tree of life. We, too, find ourselves squeezed in the wine press of life's many challenges. Mother Nature will not squeeze us until we are ripe and ready. She knows that the juice of green fruit does not taste good. The universe is patient to wait day in and day out for the fruit to ripen, until the juice is ready to harvest. You, too, must also be ready for your spirit to flow.

Fruits quickly come and go. They have a short life span. They do not waste time. They blossom... they give their juice... and then they die. Life is just as precious and just as fragile. While you are alive and blossoming, enjoy the journey. Seize the day. Always squeeze every drop out of every moment. Live life to the fullest. Are you ripe? Are you ready? Just like the little teapot, tip yourself over and pour yourself out.

Don't stay on the tree for too long. Fruit left on the vine beyond its time, decays and rots. Fruit left on the tree that does not deliver its juice fulfills no purpose. Don't waste your life. Don't hang around vegetating as a couch potato. Go out on a limb. Pick yourself up and dust yourself off. Go out into the world to fulfill your purpose. Refresh those who are thirsty. Be a healing elixir to those who are dry and parched. Pour the nectar of your heart into everything that you do.

I Feel Squeezed When I: _____

MAP YOUR

☐ STEP 11

People Who Inspired Me:
_____
_____

STOP Difficulties That Caused Me To Grow:
_____
_____

STOP

STOP Miracles That Saved Me:
_____
_____

STOP Times That I Felt Discouraged:
_____
_____

STOP Experiences That Brought Me Closer To God:
_____
_____

STOP Goals That I Reached:
_____
_____

"There are no limits... there are only plateaus.
You must not stay there.
You must rise above." - Bruce Lee

JOURNEY

What is your destination? Do you know where you are headed? Do you know where you are now? Ok, you know that you cannot go back and change the past... You are also afraid to look ahead to where you are going, because the future can be unpredictable.

So what do you do? What is your only choice? You must look at where you are right now. You must embrace what you're doing and who you're doing it with. You must create an action right now, right where you are.

There is a law, that for every action there is an equal reaction.

Your only escape from your current situation and location is to do something from where you are right now. Stop worrying about the future and stop fretting about the past. The past is gone and the future does not exist.

Now is the time. Now , right now in this moment, you have the power to create... to create a new you... to create a new life. Like Siri, the universe is waiting for you to type in your next destination. Don't be embarrassed about where you are now. Just like Siri, God doesn't care.

In a car, Siri handles all of the details. In life, the universe will give you step by step directions to your desired destination. Pay attention. Don't get distracted. Don't text and drive at the same time. Put down your phone. Stop and be still. Listen to the GPS inside of you. It will tell you what to do and where to go.

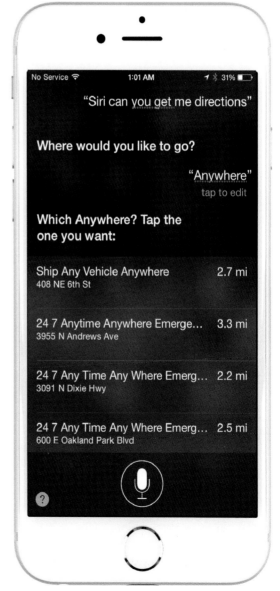

Buckle Your THE FORCE

To continue to do the same old thing and expect different results is the definition of insanity. Just take a step in a forward direction. One step... any step... do something, do anything. Don't keep going in circles. It leads to nowhere. Just one step on a path that is in a straight line will lead you away from where you are now.

It doesn't have to be a giant leap. Baby steps will get you there as well. The smallest change can make a huge difference. A tiny drop of water that drips into a crack in a rock seems like no big deal. But, watch what happens, if the weather changes, and the water freezes and turns to ice. That same drop of water, now as ice, will have the power to crack open and break apart the rock. The tiny powerless drop of water was transformed by the power of the universe. What steps do you need to take to begin to solidify your tiny drop of a dream into a solid powerful plan?

You are not alone. You are not in your current situation by yourself. In the movie, Star Wars, there is a "force" that is with you. The source of that force is from the light. The light must be integrated into your soul to awaken its full power. You must train and practice like a Jedi to tap its full potential. Everyone has the force inside of them, like a dormant volcano. Jesus said that the Kingdom of God is inside of us. Sadly, most people don't seem to notice or to care.

People who ignore the force and disregard the light will continue their journey in life going in the same old circle like a merry-go-round at a carnival. Around and round you go. No hills... no thrills. Merry-go-rounds are for kids. Have the courage to hop on the rollar coaster of life, that terrifies you. Yes, it will be a bumpy ride. Ok, its gonna take your breath away. But you will also soar to new heights. You might laugh out loud. You probably will also scream. That's ok. That's part of the fun.

27   I Will Break My Bad Habit Of: _____

Seatbelt...

AWAKENS

Tell your old shadow buddy "fear" to sit down and buckle its seat belt because you are on the ride of your life. This is the big one! This is what you have been waiting for! No more circles. No more ring-around-the-rosie. Grow up! Get ready!

Take a deep breath. Close your eyes... now open them. You are now at the top of the roller coaster. Look at how high you are. Now you can see, what you could not see from the horse seat on the carousel. From the top, you can now see where you are going. Can you see your dream from way up there? The adrenaline you feel is the force awakening inside of you. Feel the rush... feel the fun... feel the fear... feel the joy.

FEAR IS THE PATH TO THE DARK SIDE
-Yoda from Star Wars

THINK THIN

STEP 13

There is a reason why the word "diet" contains the word D-I-E in it. No one wants to live on the exhausting yo-yo of weight watching. The mind can make you healthy or sick... strong or weak... skinny or fat. Mind control IS weight control. Skinny people eat what they want and **don't** gain weight. Fat people diet and starve themselves and **do** gain weight. Thin people eat chocolate cake and fat people drink diet coke. Millions and millions of dollars are spent on diet pills and exercise equipment, but the battle of the bulge rages on.

No other step on this journey to discovering you is more life changing than this one. Discovering that you have the power in your mind to change your metabolism, by what you think while you eat, will revolutionize the shape of your body. It is not the type of food that you eat or don't eat that matters, but rather, it is the thoughts that you think as you eat the food.

Research has proven that fat people feel guilty when they eat. Surveys have even revealed that people who are overweight experience fear and paranoia while eating. In their minds, they have created food as an enemy, and weight control as a war. They feel angry when they diet, and they feel guilty when they indulge. Obesity is a eating disorder, just like anorexia and bulimia. Young girls with emaciated bodies still possess fat minds. Binging and purging food... gaining and losing weight... are conflicts in the mind, as well as in the body. Eating disorders are mental disorders. If you expect to gain weight when you eat, you will. You become what you think, therefore, be careful what you allow yourself to ponder and contemplate.

My Ideal Weight: _____

My Current Weight: _____

I can't stop eating!
I eat because I'm unhappy.. and I'm unhappy..because I eat.
- Fat Bastard (Austin Powers)

The solution is simple, CHANGE YOUR MIND ABOUT FOOD! Train your brain to think like a skinny person. Stop your love/hate relationship with food. Discipline your mind to feel relaxed and confident as you eat, instead of anxious and guilty. Eat only when you are hungry and not when you are bored. Eat to satisfy your appetite and not to escape from your emotions. Recognize cravings and addictions to sugar and caffeine, as the same mental crutch as drugs and alcohol. Don't do two things at once. Don't eat and drive, or eat and watch TV, or eat and work. The mind can only process one concept at a time. Stop what you are doing, in order to feel the satisfaction of food. Never eat on the run.

Your body is a billboard sign that advertises your thought life. Balanced thinking creates symmetrical curves. Gloomy despondent moods cannot be cured by ice cream binges. Take back control of your figure, by regaining control of your thoughts. Don't feel remorse or regret after you eat. Negative emotions hinder digestion, block assimilation and stop up elimination of food passing through your body.

Finally, the first recorded relationship between God and man took place in a garden of food. While in that paradise, the first recorded conflict between human and divine was about eating an apple. Thousands of years later, our flesh and our spirit still have the potential to be divided or united as one. By reconnecting the thoughts in the mind, with the digestion in the body, you will regain control of your garden paradise of life... and food will become once again what it was meant to be.... the fruit of heaven on earth!

FIND YOUR HAPPY

A young reporter from America traveled to one of the dirtiest slums in New Delhi for a documentary about poor people in the world. Arriving in a refugee shanty town, she was amazed to witness thousands of families living in cardboard boxes for shelter and cooking rice in fire pits for food. As she wandered from person to person, looking for someone to interview, she was even more amazed that everyone that she encountered had a

smile on their face.

Children were playing with sticks in the streets, and mothers were cheerfully washing ragged clothes in the stream next to their shacks. How could this be? Didn't these families know that they were poor! Where was the misery? Where was the suffering? There was nothing unusual or extraordinary that was worthy of a documentary about deprived, underprivileged people. On the contrary, everyone seemed abnormally happy and content.

The reporter interviewed an elderly grandmother sitting outside on the ground, playing with her grandchildren. The old woman began asking the reporter questions about America. "Tell me," she said. "I hear that in America, people do not know the names of their neighbors. How can this be? How do you help each other, if you don't even know each other?" The reporter became speechless. The old woman continued. " I also hear that families in your country get up every morning and leave each other. Is it true that fathers go one way, mothers go a different way, and children go their own way? Aren't the families sad to be apart? I certainly would not want to live there." The reporter did not know how to respond. The interview ended, and the documentary was scratched. The reporter decided to change the focus of her story.

"*Happy* girls are the **prettiest.**"
-Audrey Hepburn

The new documentary would report the fact that physical poverty does not automatically make you mentally or emotionally poor. The new story would document that the lack of money would not mean the lack of happiness. On the contrary, the new report exposed America with stories of sad scattered families, living in neighborhoods with strangers. The new documentary revealed that beautiful homes and large bank accounts did not necessarily create the paradise of Nirvana. The smiles of the New Delhi refugees would become a witness against the propaganda of a western middle-class Utopia.

Has our society traveled to the outer limits of space to explore the world, but failed to recognize the importance of the journey to the very center of our existence... the universe of our own soul. Have we discovered the path to explore the surfaces of distant planets, but have forgotten the path to discover the core of our own heart? Have we found fame and fortune, but in the process lost ourselves and our connection to each other?

Change your story. Change the documentary of your own life's journey. Travel inside to the universe of your authentic self. Discover the source of the smiles of the refugees in New Delhi. Discover the smile inside of the real you.

I Smile The Most When I: _____

DARE 2

One of the most popular songs of all time is a simple little song called, "Row Your Boat." Now, it never reached the top forty on the pop charts... And it's not exactly a Rock 'N Roll classic... however, the lyrics of that song should be the philosophy of everyone's life. In case you've never heard the little tune, it goes something like this:

> *"Row, Row, Row Your Boat,*
> *gently down the stream.*
> *Merrily, merrily, merrily,*
> *Life is but a DREAM."*

OK, it's not Beethoven or Mozart. It's certainly not a Beatle's classic... But wait a minute... Could that have been what Paul McCartney meant when he was inspired to write these words? *"When I Find Myself In Times Of Trouble Mother Mary Comes To Me, Speaking Words Of Wisdom... Let It Be."* Or maybe "Row Your Boat" inspired Sting to write the haunting lyrics: *"My soul is in a cage, swim to the light. Swim to the light."* If you listen carefully to the message behind the lyrics of many great songs, the message is the same. There is "A Bridge Over Troubled Water"... You see the same message in great art work.

The reason the Mona Lisa, by Da Vinci, became so famous was that she dared to SMILE in such a dark age of a troubled world. Why was she smiling? Did she know the secret? Is there a lost lesson that our fast paced culture has overlooked? Is there a subliminal message in the song, "Row Your Boat?" Well, let's examine each line of that song and see if it can apply to your family, your work, your friends, your health, your finances, and most importantly your own personal smile.

"Row Row Row,"
life is labor. No one is born to sit on a mountain and meditate. To create, to produce, and to work is an instinct. Watch the world around you. Notice how the ants toil to carry loads... how the squirrels run to and fro storing nuts for the Winter, and how the bees buzz from flower to flower working for a living. So what is the point... Whistle while you work! Row, Row, Row!

"Gently Down The Stream."
OK, so you are not a salmon. Quit trying to swim upstream. Go with the flow. Life should not be a struggle.

Some have made this life way too hard. Some have turned their dream into a nightmare! People who battle food and suffer through diets are usually over weight. Tight wads, misers, and stingy people usually end up broke. People who struggle to be holy and religious on the outside, usually are not very spiritual on the inside. People who don't like blood should not train to be a doctor. People who are tone deaf should not train to be a musician. Pick an occupation that utilizes all of your strengths and talents. Do you smile when you think about your job? Do you whistle while you work? Why not? So what is the answer? Men have searched for centuries in vain attempts to find real happiness and failed. Even Indiana Jones chased clues around the world for 4 movies and never quite found success. So what can the Mona Lisa and you both have in common? Find a reason to smile!

Merrily... Merrily... Merrily...
Why? Because... life is good. Think about it. The Ark of the Covenant is not hidden under a stone, or buried in a deep cave. It is inside of us. In the Wizard of Oz, Dorothy could never

DAYDREAM!

find the answer in the Emerald City. So what was it? What did she discover in the end? The Wizard certainly did not have it. The answer to her destiny was in her heart all along. She alone had the power to regain her lost happiness. Like Indiana Jones and Dorothy, the SMILE has been inside of you the whole time and you didn't know it was there. Your dormant volcano of power has been waiting to erupt and explode over your circumstances. The power does not come from your bank account or your resume'. Success has nothing to do with winning or landing a job. *Real* happiness comes from knowing that deep inside of you there is a light. Below the mere surface of your personality, there is a powerful connection that you feel to a source that is stronger than you! It's difficult to feel the connection in a crowd or above the noise. The next time you are alone, listen to your heart. The next time you are afraid, be still, be silent, and wait for it...

Life is but a *dream!*

My Wildest Dream Is:

_____

"I dream for a living."

-Steven Spielberg

The Climb

Step 3: _____

Step 2: _____

To Reach My Goal To: _____

I Will Take Step 1: _____

STEP #1:
Let It Go

You cannot control what happens moment by moment, but you can control how you react to what happens to you. For example: consider two people riding a roller coaster. One person thinks I AM enjoying this. I AM loving this... thereby releasing endorphins into their body, which creates a positive fun experience. Another person sitting next to him, thinks I AM NOT enjoying this. I AM afraid... thereby releasing adrenaline into the body, which creates a negative, terrifying experience. The roller coaster ride is the same for both people. It is their thinking reaction to the experience that is the difference.

STEP #2:
Walk Your Talk

Discipline yourself to put action behind every thought. I can say I AM an athlete every day, but if I do not make myself do something athletic everyday with that thought, I AM only fooling myself. I can say I AM thin and healthy everyday, but if I purposely eat ice cream every day, my words are wasted. Faith without works is dead.

Your talk must become your walk. Actions always speak louder than words to your subconscious mind. The thought of I AM unsuccessful... is usually followed by actions of sleeping in and wasting time. The thought of I AM successful... is usually followed by actions of rising early with enthusiasm and unstoppable excitement for productivity.

STEP #3:
Never Give Up

Several publishing companies turned down JK Rolling's Harry Potter books. She didn't give up. She persevered and became the first author to become a billionaire. Bloomingdale's originally said no to a young unknown designer with wide ties, but eventually changed their mind, allowing Ralph Lauren to sell ties in their store. Decades later, his brand name is one of the most prestigious labels in the world. Sylvester Stallone's script, "Rocky," was rejected dozens of times. He hung in there, just like his fictitious character, and he, too, became a champion making blockbuster movies. All of these people have one thing in common... They did not see failure as an obstacle. They saw it as an opportunity to pull success from within. Everyone hears the word, "no," many times. Rejection is a part of the process. "Yes" is just around the corner. Don't stop. Don't quit. Don't give up.

"Actions... not words!" - George Washington

BECOME A DIVERGENT

☐ STEP 17

So who are the people with the real power? Where are the people who do not have to create artificial power with force? Real men and women of power are rarely documented by history, because they do not seek fame or fortune. Unlike politicians and celebrities who thrive on popularity, real powerful people avoid the spotlight. Unlike bullies and jerks who try to generate artificial power by feeling superior to regular people, real powerful people are usually humble and anonymous. Every generation produces many saints and avatars whose power is documented by legend and folklore.

In our generation, Mother Teresa is an example of a shining light of humility, who did not have to use force to have power to change the world.

Unfortunately, powerful people usually have to become divergent. Divergents are people who have the courage to step off of the normal path of the majority to blaze new trails for themselves. They follow their hearts and their instincts, rather than following the opinions of the crowd. The movie, "Divergent," brought to light the dangers of challenging the rules of force. Divergents are labeled as rebels who threaten the society. In the movie, the crowds followed the majority path without question, disregarding their own personal intellect and emotions. Everyone received a shot in their neck that kept them in a walking coma.

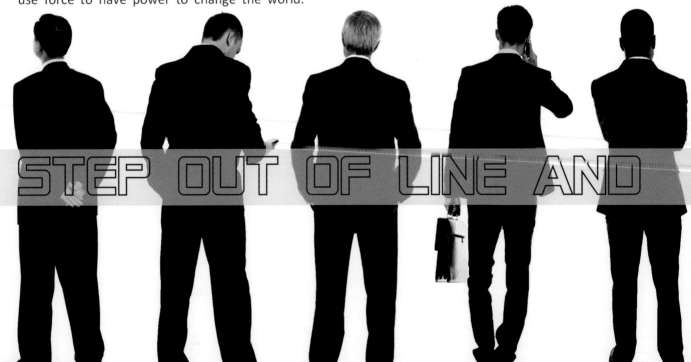

STEP OUT OF LINE AND

Is our society today similar to that movie? Do most people today blindly follow the path that is set before them, never questioning their own intuition and instincts? Are most Americans like the "Walking Dead" who sleepwalk through life. People go to work.... go to sleep... go to work... go to sleep... Are we now a generation of souls who are stuck in a rut, who never question where are we going? Is the shot in our necks, our daily addiction to electronics? Do computers, TV, cell phones and social media now control our opinions, politics and culture?

Are you an independent divergent? You should watch out! Do you think for yourself? You need to be careful. Divergents make society uncomfortable. Divergents make most people nervous. Divergents usually infuriate or intimidate those in authority. Divergents rock the boat. That's why they poisoned SOCRATES, they crucified JESUS, they murdered GANDHI, they assassinated MARTIN LUTHER KING, and they burned JOAN OF ARC at the stake.

"IT IS BETTER TO FAIL IN ORIGINALITY, THAN TO SUCCEED IN IMITATION."

- Michael Jackson

I Am Unique Because: _____

STAND OUT!

38

Dream

With The Big Boys

Steve Jobs became bored with college and dropped out of school. He went home, and spent his time in his garage following his heart. He became an icon. A genius does not develop from school alone. Abundant wisdom lies dormant inside of all of us. At 21 years old, Steve Jobs had made his 1st million. By 22 years old, he had made $10 million. By 23 years old, he had made $100 million. Then, he stopped counting.

Later in life, after building Apple to be one of the most prestigious brands in the world, Steve was voted out of his own company by the Board of Directors that he had previously hired to manage his company. He turned a potentially negative circumstance into a positive situation. Winners don't dwell on a loss. Winners don't give up.

So what did he do? He started over again from scratch. He developed Pixar, and launched Toy Story as the very first digitally designed animation film. His ability to win and to lose, without changing momentum, is beyond comparison. His capacity to roll with the punches makes him a role model for success. Steve Jobs followed Michaelangelo, Galileo, and Thomas Edison as one of the greatest avatars of all time.

The genius mind that was in each of them is also in you. The potential to create magic and wonder lies dormant in everyone's mind. To follow them, you must **follow your passion, focus on your goals, visualize your dream, and most of all, believe in yourself.**

"Some people **are worth** melting for." – Olaf, Frozen

Walt Disney lived life on the edge. He lived on the edge of immense wealth and financial ruin. He took all of his money numerous times and gambled everything on film projects. He won big with movie hits like Snow White and Mary Poppins. But he also lost money on box office disappointments, like Bambi and Pinocchio.

He lived on the edge of sanity and insanity. Some people called him a genius. Other people called him a dreamer. His biggest gamble was late in his life, when he bet everything that he had on swampland in Florida. During his final days, Walt would lay in his hospital bed with blueprints of Disney World posted on the ceiling. He died dreaming of a fantasy land, where the dreams that you dare to dream really do come true.

Five years after his death, at the grand opening of The Magic Kingdom, a reporter commented that it was sad, that Walt had not lived to see this day. Walt's brother, Roy, snapped back with unleashed anger, "None of us would be here today seeing any of this, if Walt had not seen this first. "Roy officially changed the name of Disney World that day to Walt Disney World, in honor of Walt's vision and dream.

I Imagine: _____

_____

"Great men **are not** born great, **they grow great.**"

– The Godfather

CREATIVITY is cultivated in stillness.
IMAGINATION is developed in silence.
GENIUS is unleashed in solitude.

Walt Disney and Steve Jobs were both divergents. These two shooting stars of humanity burned brightly while they were here on earth. Their minds of genius changed the world. Their lives of creativity will be remembered for generations. They both had humble beginnings. They both hit home runs and struck out at bat. They were ridiculed and unappreciated. They both were rejected by their peers. They followed their dreams through thick and thin. Their legends have promoted them to modern day avatars.

Who's next?

"Your time is limited, don't waste it living someone else's life. Don't be trapped by dogma, which is living the result of other people's thinking. Don't let the noise of other opinions drown your own inner voice. And most important, have the courage to follow your heart and intuition. They somehow already know what you truly want to become. Everything else is secondary."

"You are here to put a dent in the universe. Otherwise why else are we here?"

"That's because "things" only provide momentary bursts of happiness. To be happier, don't chase as many things. Chase experiences."

"Stay hungry. Stay foolish."

"Bottom line is, I didn't return to Apple to make a fortune. I've been very lucky in my life and already have one. I don't view wealth as something that validates my intelligence."

"Innovation distinguishes between a leader and a follower."

"My favorite things in life don't cost any money. It's really clear that the most precious resource we all have is time."

Think Like JOBS

"There is no reason not to follow your heart."

"Your work is going to fill a large part of your life, and the only way to be truly satisfied is to do what you believe is great work. And the only way to do great work is to love what you do. If you haven't found it yet, keep looking. Don't settle. As with all matters of the heart, you'll know when you find it."

"It's better to be a pirate than to join the Navy.."

"Being the richest man in the cemetery doesn't matter to me. Going to bed at night saying we've done something wonderful, that's what matters to me."

"Sometimes life is going to hit you in the head with a brick. Don't lose faith."

"We don't get a chance to do that many things, and every one should be really excellent. Because this is our life. Life is brief, and then you die, you know? And we've all chosen to do this with our lives. So it better be damn good. It better be worth it."

Put A Star Next To Your Favorite Quote.

"That's the real trouble with the world, too many people grow up."

"You reach a point where you don't work for money."

"Crowded classrooms and half-day sessions are a tragic waste of our greatest national resource, the minds of our children."

"The more you like yourself, the less you are like anyone else, which makes you unique."

"Disneyland is a work of love. We didn't go into Disneyland just with the idea of making money."

"Laughter is timeless, imagination has no age, and dreams are forever.

"Never stop dreaming."

43

Think Like DISNEY

"I only hope that we don't lose sight of one thing - that it was all started by a mouse."

"It's kind of fun to do the impossible."

"You may not realize it when it happens, but a kick in the teeth may be the best thing in the world for you.""

"Why worry? If you've done the very best you can. Worrying won't make it any better."

"Everyone falls down. Getting back up is how you learn how to walk."

"In bad times and in good, I have never lost my sense of zest for life."

First, think. Second, believe. Third, dream. And finally, dare.

"Happiness is a state of mind. It's just according to the way you look at things."

If you can dream it, you can do it.

"All our dreams can come true, if we have the courage to pursue them."

"I've heard there is going to be a recession. I've decided not to participate. "

Make A Wish!

Imagination: The Genie In The Bottle

There are two different ways to see. One is called sight, created by your eyeballs. The other is called vision, created by your mind. Sight is what you see now, in the present. It is what is in front of your face. Whereas, vision is what is seen in the future. It is what your mind can imagine. Just like a genie in a bottle, your imagination can take a simple wish and send It on a magic carpet ride. Before there was the Internet, Bill Gates had a vision of a whole new electronic world. He used his imagination and creativity to bring it into our eyesight. Before there was the light bulb, Thomas Edison envisioned it, imagined it. He spent his entire life developing his dream to bring light to the darkness. Before we went to the moon, John Kennedy envisioned man's footprints in lunar sand and challenged America to achieve the impossible.

In my own example, years before I had the sight of my children with my eyeballs.... I had a vision of them in my mind and in the imagination of my heart. Even as a young girl, I would play with baby dolls and fantasize about being a mother. Then one day, I turned around, and there they were... just as I had imagined them to be.

Catwalk Productions existed for years in my mind, before the first model ever walked the runway.

At first, my catwalks were simple homemade stages made of plywood. However, I never stopped dreaming of a beautiful stage with runway lights. Eventually, my fashion show stages were featured on MTV network to showcase international designers. But it all started with a simple dream. It grew with a vision. It became reality with my imagination. Do you have a vision? Do you ever daydream? Make a wish. The day by day path of your imagination is the dream unfolding before your eyes. Seize the moment.

Don't waste your vision by imagining bad things happening in your future. That's called fear. Don't waste your vision by plotting revenge or making plans to get even. That is called a complete waste of time. Begin right now to create a vision of what you want in your future... good health... good fortune... Whatever it is, just be very specific. Vague vision, just like poor eyesight, will cause you to run into walls. Do you have a vision for your daily schedule? What is your goal for every day? DREAM BIG! Your vision is the train. Your imagination is the track. Just like Jasmine and Aladdin, take your imagination on a magic carpet ride.

If I Had A Genie In A Bottle, My Three Wishes Would Be:

1. _____

2. _____

3. _____

"Imagine. People say that I'm a dreamer... Maybe someday you will join us, and the world will live as one."
-John Lennon

48

FLOW TO GROW

☐ **STEP 22** Some people seem to flow through life, and other people obviously struggle every day. People who flow, smile a lot. People who struggle, complain constantly. People who flow seem to be anointed with the talents they need to accomplish the tasks. People who struggle blame other people or circumstances for their inability to produce.

LeBron James and Carrie Underwood are both examples of people who flow. Both of them work by the sweat of their brow... but neither of them struggle to produce. Carrie simply opens her mouth and her gift of song flows. LeBron runs up and down the court under tremendous pressure to produce, but it seems that he welcomes the opportunity to shoot a three pointer at the final buzzer.

Working hard and enjoying what you do is flowing. Working hard and being miserable about what you do is struggling.

No river flows in a straight line. It twists and turns with the hills and valleys of the land. The water current changes speed and direction as needed with no resistance. Water that does not flow, becomes stagnant. People who do not flow, get stuck in the mud. In life, your ability to also change course will enable you to go with the flow. People and circumstances block your flow everyday.

Through the years, I have learned to flow. I have lived in a shack. I have lived in a mansion. Different houses... same me. I have felt the ecstasy of holding a newborn baby and felt the horror of burying one. Different emotions... same me. I have known the thrill of victory and the agony of defeat. Different results... same me.

Close your eyes... and breathe deeply for two minutes. Breathe in strength, health, success, and joy. Breathe out anger, dysfunction, disease and discontent. Feel the flow... Watch you grow.

I Am The Happiest When: _____

_____

" Far better it is to dare to do mighty things...
to win,and to learn from
glorious triumphs and
devastating failures... than to rank with those
poor spirits who neither enjoy nor suffer
much, because they live in the
gray twilight that knows neither
victory
nor defeat."
-Theodore Roosevelt

48

BE the BUTTERFLY

i am looking for a lot of men who have the infinite capacity to believe the impossible.

-Henry Ford

49

EFFECT

There was a tribe of people in Africa who complained about their rocky, stony soil which was horrible farmland. They fumed and fretted every year, trying to make crops grow on their terrible fields. After years of anger and depression, the tribe's leaders decided to pull up stakes and move the tribe hundreds of miles away.

Afterward, another tribe moved into the area and also encountered the rocky soil. Instead of complaining, they decided to create a solution to their own problem. They discovered that the soil was able to produce grassy pastures good enough for sheep grazing. They learned to be prosperous on the land in spite of the rocks.

A young shepherd boy from the tribe put one of the stones from the fields in his pocket. One day, he was hitting the stone with a stick at a nearby trading post. A man noticed that the boy's shiny stone was actually a diamond. The rocky soil was actually dirt filled with diamonds! These fields are known today as the Kimberly Mines in South Africa, the richest plot of land on the face of the earth. What was a curse to one tribe became a blessing to the next tribe!

Before taking your next step, look around where you are standing. Your greatest treasure may already be right beside you. Some people see thorns. Other people see a rose. Quit trying to save the world and first just save yourself. Stop dwelling on what you can't do and focus on what you can do. Just like a butterfly who effortlessly flaps its wings, you can create ripple effects that are beyond your wildest imagination. Circle one thing that you can do today to change your world.

Things I Cannot Do To Save The World:

- Solve the budget deficit
- Take away world hunger
- Create national health care
- Reverse global warming
- Negotiate peace in the Middle East
- Find a cure for aids
- Stop domestic violence
- Change my age or my height
- Control the price of gas
- Make it rain in California

Things I Can Do To Save The World:

- Give the waiter a nice tip
- Quit smoking
- Smile at a stranger for no reason
- Hold the door open for the person behind you
- Forgive somebody who hurt me
- Be kind to my neighbor
- Take time to talk to my grandmother
- Write a positive comment on Facebook
- Walk away from an argument
- Compliment my co worker in the next cubicle

Believe that you CAN

Challenges can create heroes, or create cowards. Obstacles can boost you higher or they can pull you down. What is in your way? What is keeping you from reaching your goal? Aim for the truth. Follow the feeling in your gut. Listen to the voice in your head. If it is a positive vibe, you are listening to your spirit. If it is a negative vibe, then you are listening to your ego.

The soul says, "yes." The personality says, "no." The divine in you says, "You can do it." The mortal in you says, "Don't even try." Optimism comes from the light. Pessimism originates from a dark place.

Life is a balancing act between the two forces inside of you. One force is a winner... the other a loser. We all have the potential to be one or the other.

We all have two wolves living inside of us. One wolf is daring and courageous. The other wolf is weak and fearful. Which wolf will survive? Which wolf do you keep? Which wolf needs to leave? Which one do you feed? Your thoughts become the wolves' food. The one that is fed is the one that grows. The one that starves, goes away. Feed your spirit... Feed your truth.

I Believe That I Can: _____

_____

"When I auditioned
for the movie, King Kong,
I was told that I was not attractive enough
to play the leading lady. I went home, and had the choice
to listen to what the casting director said.. or, to believe in myself.

I pulled myself up by the bootstraps., and decided to believe in me.
Since losing that audition, I have since been nominated for 19 academy awards."
-Meryl Streep

□ STEP 25

Be -YOU-

I am an author. Sometimes, I wake up at 4:30 in the morning... just to write! Isn't that crazy? Well it would be, if I didn't have the passion to put thoughts into words on paper. Other people get up before dawn to work out, because they have a passion to be an athlete. On the other hand, some people sleep in and find no good reason to get out of bed. Their job does not give them the energy to wake up. Their life does not stimulate them to get up and get going.

Everyone, let me repeat, everyone has a gift. Your gift is your talent. It is the source of an ability to do something extremely well. The ability to cook or to dance... or the talent to play a sport or paint a picture, are all examples of God Given Gifts. Our gift is usually also our passion. Rock stars sing in the shower and artists doodle on paper. Real talent cannot be bought through lessons. It cannot be faked or imitated.

My granddaughters could take years of voice lessons and never sing like Taylor Swift. My sons tried for years to be like Mike practicing basketball, hoping to be the next Michael Jordan. Unfortunately, they were not born with his gift.

Taylor or Michael do not struggle to use their abilities. Rather, there is a natural flow or non-resistance to what they do.

So you think you're cute... Get over yourself. Pretty faces are a dime a dozen. Take the time to think about your real gift. Stop and consider what you are good at and what you enjoy doing. What skill do you perform naturally? Have you ever said, "I would do that for free?" Maybe that is your clue to what you are really supposed to be doing. Find your authentic self. If you continue to fake your job, or pretend in your relationship; you will eventually burn out. You will simply wear yourself down. When you genuinely use your skills and gifts, you will draw from a well-spring of energy. When you are in the right relationship, you will have a peace of mind that is genuine.

Every day, take one step in the direction of your heart. Every day, take 1 step away from the situation that makes you struggle. Slowly, little by little, with every step in the right direction, you will feel the difference. You will breathe easier. You will discover your beautiful self.

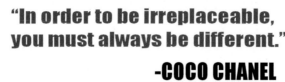

"In order to be irreplaceable, you must always be different."
-COCO CHANEL

53 I Am Fabulous When I: _____

54

Mastermind Your Life

There was an old miner who had dug for copper for 20 yrs. One day his beloved mule stepped in a gopher hole and broke his leg. The miner realized that his long time partner must be shot and put down. Instead of giving in to discouragement and depression, the old man sang as he remembered the years of their ups and downs together as a team. As he dug the grave for his faithful mule, the miner struck the largest vein of copper that he had ever discovered; thus, escalating him to much wealth. Sometimes your greatest success lies just beyond your greatest failures.

☐ **STEP 26**

Do you really believe in yourself? Do you really believe that you have a goal to reach that is worth your passion?

Before you take the next step, reflect on who you are and what you want to do. A calm lake reflects the light of the full moon when it is peaceful and

still. Turbulent waters fail to capture the image of what is above. Begin your master plan by being still. Sit in silence. Your next step will reflect the thoughts in your mind. Don't go forward with a turbulent mind. Wait for the waters of your mind to calm down... THEN GO FOR IT!

Develop a strong will and stubborn determination that will out weigh any failure that comes against you. If you get knocked down, get back up again. Fail miserably but try again. The harder the problem, the deeper you have to dig to find the inspiration to face it. Remember, the old man was a miner who searched for great treasures like copper and gold, hidden beneath the surface of the earth. We, too, must also learn to mine great treasures like courage and perseverance, that are hidden deep within our own soul. Most people have untapped resources and gifts that are lying dormant deep within themselves.

Once you have MINED your hidden resources, your positive attitude will be your rocket fuel to lift you above any circumstance. You can be the avatar of your destiny. Seek and ye shall find... Ask and you shall receive... There is a force inside of you that is knocking on the door of your heart. Have the courage to open the door. Keep digging... keep searching... mastermind your life. Make goals and plans for your future. You might just be inches away from your treasure.

My Master Plan Is: _____

_____

Fill In The Blank

I Am _____.

As children, we all dreamed of growing up to be somebody special. Our labor defines our abilities. I AM an artist.... I AM a salesmen... I AM a teacher... When you finally say I AM a _____ with confidence, you will begin the journey of discovering your destiny. Finding your true calling in life is to find your true destiny here on Earth. Discovering your true gift is the adventure of a lifetime. The following people knew who they were and where they were going. Our ability to define who we are is what makes us extra-ordinary. Do you know who you are?

"Be who you are... not who the world wants you to be."
- Captain America

"*I AM* not afraid. I was born to do this." - Joan of Arc

"*I AM* who I AM and say what I think." - Eminem

"*I AM* prepared to die, but there is no cause for which I AM prepared to kill." - Gandhi

"*I AM* still Jenny from the block. I used to have a little, now I have a lot. - JLo

"*I AM* a pencil in the hand of a God who is sending a love letter to the world." - Mother Teresa

"*I AM* the way, the truth, and the life." - Jesus of Nazareth

"*I AM* my own experiment. I AM my own work of art." - Madonna

"*I AM* the toughest golfer mentally in the world." - Tiger Woods
"*I AM* an artist that draws freely upon my imagination." - Albert Einstein
"*I AM* always trying that which I cannot do." - Pablo Picasso
"*I AM* seeking and striving with all of my heart." - Vincent Van Gogh
"*I AM* where I AM because I believe in all possibilities." - Whoopi Goldberg
"*I AM* not funny... What I AM is brave." - Lucille Ball
"*I AM* the greatest... I said that even before I knew I was." - Muhammad Ali
"*I AM* awake." - Buddha
"*I AM.*" - God

Don't Try
To Be
Something
You're Not

Do What You Love

Everyone's choice of occupation or career usually defines deep down inside of them who they really are. For example, a nurse is compassionate. A soldier has to be courageous. And an astronaut is usually daring and adventurous. Young models advertise jeans, and older models advertise metamucil. If your current job leaves you empty and unfulfilled, maybe it's time to pursue a career that dares you to dream. A dream motivates you to achieve greatness. A job gives you a paycheck, and pays your bills. A dream makes you successful and satisfied. A job is boring and monotonous. Is your job a dream job? Your work develops your talents and skills. Unfortunately, most jobs don't. Your job should pay you in proportion to your production. Most jobs do not.

Most people fall into two categories for careers. Dreamers live to work, while most people work to live. Some people hate their job. They wait for TGIF every week. They dread getting out of bed to go to work. Hitting the snooze button on their alarm is a part of their morning routine. Monday morning is a dreaded curse word in their vocabulary.

"I want to do it **because** I want to do it."
- Amelia Earheart

Love What

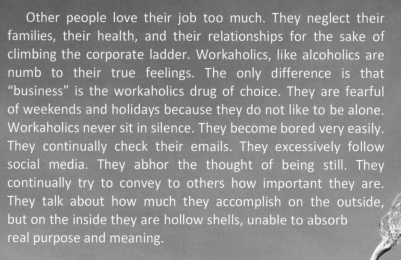

Other people love their job too much. They neglect their families, their health, and their relationships for the sake of climbing the corporate ladder. Workaholics, like alcoholics are numb to their true feelings. The only difference is that "business" is the workaholics drug of choice. They are fearful of weekends and holidays because they do not like to be alone. Workaholics never sit in silence. They become bored very easily. They continually check their emails. They excessively follow social media. They abhor the thought of being still. They continually try to convey to others how important they are. They talk about how much they accomplish on the outside, but on the inside they are hollow shells, unable to absorb real purpose and meaning.

Vincent Van Goch would sit and paint for hours and hours. He never sold a single picture! No one ever appreciated his genius talent. Sadly, he committed suicide when he was 33 years old. His final painting was a sunset with a note attached, "My work is done."

Work alone will not fulfill your purpose in life. Talent is only a piece of the puzzle. Measure every task that you do with a joy barometer. Find your happy place and create your life forward from there.

My Favorite Thing To Do Is: _____

You Do

WITHOUT LIFE'S UPS AND DOWNS...

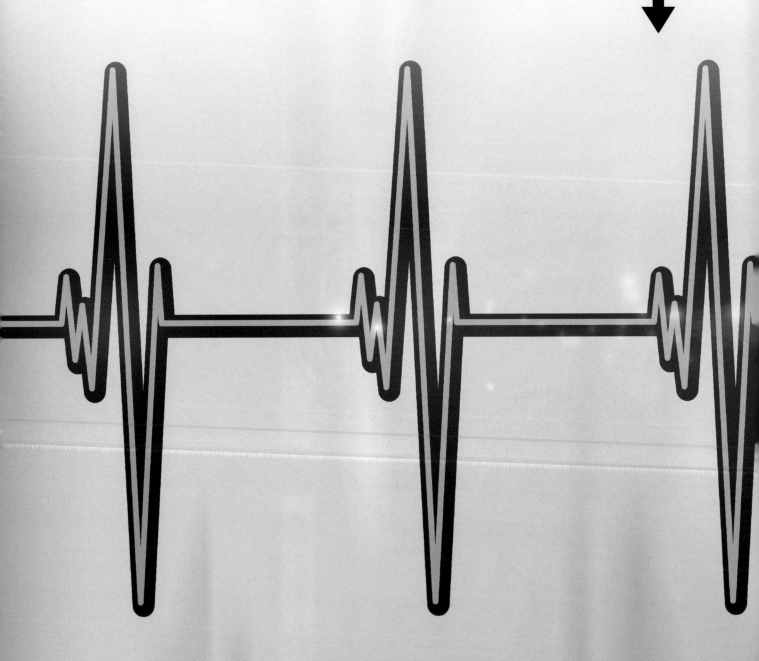

...YOU WOULD BE DEAD.

"YOUR TIME IS LIMITED,
so don't waste it living someone else's life."
- Steve Jobs

FIND

61

THE TRUTH

As kids, we all played the game of "Truth or Dare." Players had the choice to tell the truth or take a risk. Daring to take a risk was usually only funny or embarrassing, but because it was just a game, it was always harmless.

In life however, failing to choose the truth can be devastating and horrendous. "The truth will set you free," is not just a wise old saying, it should be your mantra for living.

Lies and illusions are polar opposites of truth and reality. The following chart illustrates the choices each of us have to make everyday. Choose truth and you take a step toward the light. Choose illusions and you take a step into darkness.

Truth or Dare? Each of our feelings and thoughts propel us on or off of our path. Illusions create a cartoon caricature of who we really are. Grow up like Pinocchio and play to win.... I dare you to choose the truth.

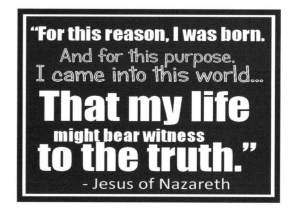

"For this reason, I was born. And for this purpose, I came into this world... That my life might bear witness to the truth."
- Jesus of Nazareth

TRUTH	⟵ CHOICES ⟶	ILLUSIONS
HEALTH	STATE	DISEASE
ABUNDANCE	SUBSTANCE	POVERTY
COURAGE	EMOTION	FEAR
GOOD	VIBRATION	EVIL
GOD	SOURCE	DEVIL
WISDOM	CONSCIOUSNESS	IGNORANCE
FREEDOM	POTENTIAL	LIMITATION
FLOW	MOTION	STAGNATION
POWER	ABILITY	WEAKNESS

Unleash The X Factor

Have you ever heard of the term, the x factor? Yes, I know it's a talent show. But do you know what the "x" factor really means? When we audition models for Pose Magazine, we look for the model who has "it." Auditions are usually looking for the one who has the ability to stand out in a crowd. Castings are searching for the one with the x factor.

The "x" is the intersecting point of two lines. It is in the center of the combination of both lines. The X is the sweet spot. **A person is an intersection of both a body and a soul.** Two lines can either run parallel or intersect. Those, whose body intersects with their soul have the x factor. When the body and the soul connect there is magic.

Soul music is music that transcends the voice box alone. It comes from a connection to a deeper source. Soul food goes beyond the palette. It also feeds your spirit. The church symbolizes the x factor with the cross. Man and God... body and spirit intersecting at Calvary.

When the part of you that is mortal intersects with the part of you that is divine, you create ground zero for an explosion of creation. The intersection of heaven and earth is the fusion of God's spirit with man's personality.

Champion athletes talk about being "in the zone," when they achieve seemingly impossible abilities to make the shot or win the game. What zone are they talking about? The Twilight Zone? Well, maybe. Twilight is the time between daylight and nightfall.

It is the moment when the light of day intersects with the darkness of night. In legends and folklore, twilight is the mystical time of magic. The sunrise and sunset have always captured our imagination.

To discover your x factor, find your twilight zone. Find you own sweet spot. Feel and experience the intersection of your own light and darkness. When the lack and limitation of your flesh meets the freedom and the abundance of your spirit, you too will find the zone. You will achieve things beyond your natural abilities. You will accomplish the impossible. **You will discover the eye of the tiger...** the intersection of finite with infinity.

If the human line never intersects with the divine, it will drift off into psychosis and mental illness. When flesh intersects with spirit, the body experiences harmony and balance. The x factor describes someone that has achieved "nirvana." That someone is one who seems to transcend life in a mystical and mysterious way.

In mathematics, x represents the unknown. The equation can now be solved. The answer is clear. Michaelangelo discovered the secret of the x factor and painted the Renaissance Man during the dark ages. The x factor is the intersection of your personality and your spirit. To end up on the right road to discover yourself, make sure to travel through the intersection of your own "x" factor.

My Spirit Wants: _____

My Flesh Wants: _____

"GOD MADE MAN IN HIS OWN IMAGE... MALE AND FEMALE."
-The Book Of Genesis

PLUG

INTO THE SECRET

SOURCE

To discover yourself, you must become conscious of the source of all power. To uncover your purpose and destiny in life, you must learn to connect to this power with positive thoughts and good intentions. If thought is constructive, it will harness and possess vitality. Good thoughts will grow and develop into a good actions. Good actions will attract everything necessary for the completion of the purpose of the thought. Positive thoughts contain within themselves the pass codes to creativity and imagination. Good thoughts weave a garment of happiness and harmony into the web of life.

Universal power will not connect to negative thoughts and destructive intentions. If you choose thoughts of worry, stress or fear; your mind will lose connection with source, just as a cell phone loses connection with the tower signal. If the thoughts are negative, they will have within themselves the germ of dissolution, which will produce discord and destruction.

Fear is a powerful form of thought. Unconstrained stress will paralyze the circulation system of the body, affecting the brain, the muscles, and the heart.

Meditation can rewire, reverse, and restore the damage that destructive thoughts have produced. Stillness and quiet time must become a necessary part of your schedule, in the same way that a cell phone must be left alone to be charged. Electrical power is both positive and negative. It can toast a piece of bread. It can electrocute and kill a human being. Thought power also can create or destroy. A thought of kindness can lead to a good deed. A thought of hate can lead to murder.

Frustration and depression are symptoms that you have lost power. Anger and bitterness are the results of an uncharged mind that has disconnected from the power source. People who are connected to the source tower become people of destiny. People who are not connected to source tower become people of chance.

A Powerful Person That I Admire Is: _____

"Happiness Lies In The Joy Of Achievement And The Thrill Of Creative Effort."

- Franklin Roosevelt

"HOLDING ON TO **ANGER** IS LIKE HOLDING ONTO A **HOT COAL** WITH THE INTENT OF THROWING IT AT SOMEONE ELSE. **YOU ARE THE ONE** WHO WILL BE **BURNED.**"

-Buddha

RELAX & RECHARGE

☐ **STEP 33**

Electricity is the cause. A hairdryer is the effect. Electricity is the cause. A refrigerator is the effect. Electricity is the power. The light bulb is the object of the demonstration of the power.

Likewise, the universe is the cause. Rain is the effect. The universe is the cause. A new-born baby is the effect. The universe is the power. Thought is the object of the demonstration of real power.

The source of the universe's power is just as mysterious as the source of electricity. We don't have to understand the mystery in order to use it. Jesus called the source of the power to perform miracles, "Father," and considered himself the object of the demonstration of that power. Abraham, the patriarch of Judaism and Islam, called the source of power, "Jehovah." Hindus, call the source of the power of the universe, "Prana." Muslims call the universal power, "Allah."

The power of electricity moves mysteriously through inanimate objects made of metals like steal and copper. The power of the universe moves and manifests through living bodies. With the correct use of electrical power, a city can be brightly lit on the darkest of nights. With the correct use of the universal power, a human being can harness an inflow of vital energy. This energy is generated by the controlled flow of thoughts in the same way that electricity is generated by the controlled flow of water.

So here's the point. You are not the source of power. You are the object of the demonstration of the power. You are not the cell tower, you are the cell phone. You are not God, you are a child of God. You are not the whole. You are a part of the whole. You are not the cause, you are the effect. But with the right connection, you can channel the power of the divine and you can manifest the abundance of the universe.

GOT POWER? GOD POWER? GO AHEAD AND PLUG IN...
RECHARGE... RENEW... RELAX.... RECEIVE!

"It's a new dawn... IT'S A NEW DAY... and I'm feeling good."
- Michael Buble'

_____ Is My Happy Place.

DON'T RUN

Heroes use power. Villains use force. To understand the difference between the good guys and the bad guys, you must understand the difference between power and force. They are synonyms in the dictionary, but in reality, they are two completely different concepts. The sharp contrast between power and force is that power is produced, when you are plugged into the source of the universe. Force, on the other hand, is plugged into nothing. It has no source other than the ego of the mind. Power is always that of love, and force is always that of ego. Power builds and restores... Force destroys and tears down.

on when the user taps it for positive intentions. When the intention is negative, such as murder or war, the universe is unresponsive to help, aid, or assist, just like a dead uncharged battery.

Therefore, tyrants and terrorists, or anyone who produces negative thoughts, are left alone and abandoned by the power of the universe. They, then, must turn to their own abilities to generate force and authority. This force usually grows into ugly monsters with intentions to harm and destroy. The universe cannot, and will not endorse or support negativity. Therefore, negative people, whether it is a dictator or

Heroes use power. Villains use force.

Power is from spirit and force is from flesh. Force is what men have to rely on, who do not possess real power. Hitler, Stalin, and Genghis Khan are examples of weak men, who counterfeited real strength with the use of brutal force. Their lack of being plugged into the power of the universe was caused by their negative intentions. The universe is intricately good and positive. Therefore, it can only be turned

a bully, usually become more and more negative from a lack of real power. This induces more mental illness, in the form of low self esteem and inferiority complexes. Anyone can spiral into mental disorders, as the result of thinking negative thoughts instead of positive thoughts. The news reports everyday stories of crazy people; from husbands killing wives, to children murdering parents. Anyone who becomes

OUT OF TIME

☐ **STEP 34**

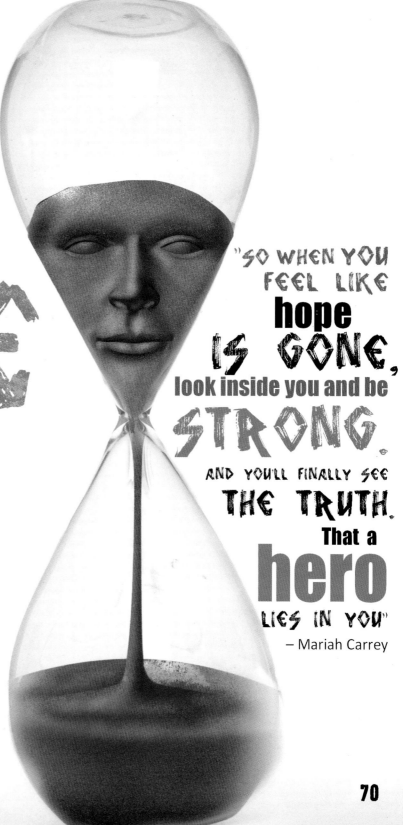

disconnected from the positive power source of the light of the universe, sadly loses their way in the darkness and eventually stumbles and falls.

Villains always run out of steam. Villains always run out of time. They eventually run down and lose power. There will always be bullies. There will always be Hitlers who rise and fall. But remember, there will also always be heroes. Heroes get stronger as they tap their infinite power source. The darkness of night is always extinguished by the dawn of a new day. The resurrection followed the crucifixion. And just like in the movies, the good guys always win in the end.

I Feel Powerful When I: _____

_____

"SO WHEN YOU FEEL LIKE **hope** IS GONE, look inside you and be STRONG. AND YOU'LL FINALLY SEE THE TRUTH. That a **hero** LIES IN YOU"
– Mariah Carrey

Surround Yourself
With
Winners

STEP 35 Peers, friends and family are the strongest influence on your life choices. An old proverb warns, "If you walk with the wise, you become wise. If you walk with fools, you will suffer harm."

Young men who need discipline, sometimes join the military to find direction. By being accountable to their Drill Sergeant, they develop new attitudes of success and self confidence. By associating with a new group that is also highly disciplined; they, too, become trained to win. Sadly, when veterans leave the military, many of them go back to their old neighborhoods and peers, only to lose their confidence once again, and return to their old way of thinking.

In the same way, if you want to become a better tennis player, you must play with players who are better than you. You will never elevate your abilities by playing with someone with less talent than you. To increase strength, you add weight. To up your game, you must go to the next level. Train forward not backwards.

Friends have the same effect. Hang out with people who are stronger, not weaker than you. If you are trying to quit drugs, don't associate with drug addicts. It is difficult to stay motivated, when you hang out with friends that are unmotivated. Find better friends who walk and talk success. Leave friends behind who mock your dreams and criticize your goals. Stay away from people who you know are a bad influence on you. Rather, you must have the courage to walk away. Develop the confidence to say, "goodbye."

"It takes a great deal of bravery to stand up to our enemies, but even more **to stand up to our friends.**"
- Harry Potter

FINANCIALLY... SPIRITUALLY... AND SOCIALLY...

you are the average of the 5 closest people that surround you.

Who are your 5 closest relationships?

1._____ 2._____ 3._____ 4. _____ 5. _____

Now rate each one of them on the scale in the following areas. Then, do the math.
Add the total of all 5 friends and divide by 5 to project what you are "creating by association."

Financial Income:

Below 20,000	20,000-50,000	50,000-100,000	100,000-150,000	above 150,000
☐☐☐☐☐	☐☐☐☐☐	☐☐☐☐☐	☐☐☐☐☐	☐☐☐☐☐

Spiritual Affiliations:

Atheist	Agnostic	Hypocrite	Religious	Spiritual
☐☐☐☐☐	☐☐☐☐☐	☐☐☐☐☐	☐☐☐☐☐	☐☐☐☐☐

Social Status:

Party Animal	Player	Divorced	Single	Married
☐☐☐☐☐	☐☐☐☐☐	☐☐☐☐☐	☐☐☐☐☐	☐☐☐☐☐

Average Financial Income: _____ **Average Spiritual Affiliation:** _____ **Average Social Status:** _____

Live
with
Passion

STEP 36

73

What Is Passion?

It means to have enthusiasm for what you are doing. In the Greek, "En" means in and "theo" means divinity. Therefore, enthusiasm conveys the notion of being one with a higher source. Another word that is similar is inspiration, or "in" the "spirit." To be inspired or to be enthusiastic about what you are doing is to be directly ordained to flow.

Passion does not necessarily mean happiness. Take for instance, a marathon runner who is going up a hill at mile fourteen! His passion, his enthusiasm, and his inspiration have to override his perspiration and lack of happiness at that moment. Happiness comes and goes. Passion endures.

To have continual passion is to possess a very deep and wide foundation of a bedrock of joy for who your are and what you're doing. Similar to the ocean, the surface may be smooth and peaceful one day and stormy and turbulent the next day. However, deep down underneath the surface, the water is always still... always calm... completely unaffected by the storm that is rocking its surface.

You must find your joy in what you are doing. Find the joy that is deep within your very soul, that is located at the center of your being. Then, you will have found your anchor that holds your life in tow. Passion originates in your soul. It is sustained in your mind. It is demonstrated in your actions.

The job alone can never satisfy you. Money will never fulfill your deepest needs. People will always disappoint you. Anyone can hurt you, if you give them the power to do so. The power belongs to you unless you give it away to someone else. Friends come and go. Keep your eyes on your goal. Don't get distracted by challenges or intimidated by obstacles.

MAKE IT HAPPEN!

Learn to play the game of life right where you are NOW, with the people next to you NOW, doing what you are doing NOW. Quit looking for passion around the next corner and find it right where you are **now.**

"I don't go by the rule book. I lead from my heart and not my head."
-Princess Diana

I Am At My Best When I: _____

STRE

Beauty really is only skin deep. Pretty people are usually branded as being shallow. Develop the ability to dig deep under your skin to find hidden wisdom and dormant talent. These treasures that are buried deep within your personality, are waiting to be tapped. You will quickly discover that your real value is not in your LOOKS, but in your CHARACTER. Your real talents will be revealed to be the foundation of your life. Pretty faces are a dime a dozen. People who rely on their looks usually are insecure with low self esteem.

Creating a healthy self image is similar to a great marketing campaign. Nike, who sells more shoes then any other company in the world, never talks about their shoes in their commercials. Instead, they align their brand name with the concept of winning. So subconsciously, when we think of the word "Nike", we automatically associate it with winning and success. Savvy advertising, huh?

Milk sales plummeted for years when their advertising tried to convince us that milk was good for us. Nobody cared! Then, someone came up with a short slogan... GOT MILK?... Suddenly, revenues reversed, and began to skyrocket. Selling the absence of milk paid off more than selling the benefits of milk. Someone once said, "Don't sell the steak, sell the sizzle." Your personality and passion, your strengths and weaknesses, all combine to create the person that you are. Part of you is, of course, shallow and materialistic. That's ok. Because part of you is also deep and spiritual. Feel comfortable in your own skin. The more you love... the more you become lovable. The more you hate... the more you become unlovable. Life is a boomerang... What you give... you get. Go ahead. Stretch yourself... and just like Nike. *Just do it!*

TCH YOURSELF

☐ **DAY 37**

1. Drink Too Much
2. Spend More Than You Make
3. Throw Temper Tantrums
4. Eat Empty Calories
5. Sleep Around
6. Curse Like A Sailor
7. Do Drugs
8. Party Late and Oversleep
9. Become Spoiled and Arrogant
10. Slip Into Bad Habits
11. Become Shallow Airheads
12. Forget Where You Came From

List two negative habits that are leading you towards failure.

1. _____
2. _____

So, how do you find your authentic self? How do you uncover the real you? The best way is to follow examples of former seekers who just like you, had to discover themselves. Moses got overwhelmed with his job, so he fled to a mountain to be alone. There in SOLITUDE, he discovered his true identity as a leader. Buddha became disillusioned with his life of luxury, so he left the palace to sit under a tree for a long time. There in STILLNESS, he uncovered his real purpose in life was to transcend suffering. Jesus needed a break from the noise of the crowds, so he escaped to the desert. There in SILENCE, he confronted his own light and his own darkness.

> "Faith in yourself is the best course." -Michaelangelo

Stretch the right way

1. Set Goals
2. Create a Healthy Lifestyle
3. Live With Passion
4. Exemplify Integrity
5. Finish What You Start
6. Balance Mind, Body, and Soul
7. Demonstrate Self Control
8. Practice Humility
9. Develop Real Relationships
10. Master Time Management
11. Spend Money Wisely
12. Train To Your Limit

List two positive habits that are leading you towards success.

1. _____
2. _____ **76**

Put the Pieces of the Puzzle TOGETHER

☐ **STEP 38**

Man is not born ready made. As a young child, he is like an uncut stone that is ready for the sculptor's hand. Through the years, man has the potential to self create or self destruct. Man has the free will to choose whether his life will become either a beautiful statue or an ugly grotesque hunk of stone. Choose your career wisely, as it can carve you into a valuable piece of art. What you do must match who you are.

I love to:_____

I will become:_____

_____

Match the DESIRE With The DO

DESIRE

I LOVE TO TRAVEL
I LOVE TO DRAW
I LOVE TO ACT
I LOVE TO BUILD THINGS
I LOVE TO CARE FOR PEOPLE
I LOVE TO WRITE
I LOVE TO ENTERTAIN
I LOVE TO WRITE POETRY
I LOVE TO CREATE
I LOVE TO PLAY THE GUITAR
I LOVE TO EXPLORE
I LOVE TO PLAY SPORTS
I LOVE TO HELP PEOPLE
I LOVE TO SELL STUFF

DO

BECOME A MISSIONARY
BECOME AN AUTHOR
BECOME A PRO ATHLETE
BECOME A MUSICIAN
BECOME AN ACTOR
BECOME A PILOT
BECOME A SONGWRITER
BECOME AN ENTREPRENEUR
BECOME AN ARCHEOLOGIST
BECOME AN ARTIST
BECOME AN ARCHITECT
BECOME A DOCTOR
BECOME A MODEL
BECOME AN INVENTOR

"**Here's to the crazy ones...** the misfits, the rebels, the trouble makers, the round pegs in the square holes... The ones who see things differently. They're not fond of rules, and they have no respect for the status quo. You can quote them, disagree with them, glorify or vilify them. But the only thing you cannot do, is ignore them. Because **they change things** and push the human race forward. While some may see them as the crazy ones... We see genius. Because **the people who are crazy** enough to think **they can change the world...** **are the ones who do.**" - Apple TV Commercial

78

EXPRESS YOURSELF!

☐ STEP 39

One of your greatest instincts in life is to express yourself. On the surface, you express yourself by the way you talk and by the way you walk. Your swag is your authentic self. Your hairdo and your fashion style, both define your personality to others without words.

Communication is an important way to learn to express yourself. Some people have replaced their own words and expressions with emojis. Who needs to have an eye to eye conversation anymore, when you can just shoot them a text? Everything that you choose to do is an expression of who you are. Writing a poem or climbing a mountain, are both examples of an outward activity, that expresses an inward desire.

Expression can be positive or negative. Graffiti on walls are an outlet for some people to express their frustration. Anger and depression are both outward manifestations of inner turmoil. Insecurity and low self esteem will hinder the flow of accurately expressing your true self.

What is holding you back?

Let go of fear and doubt. It may be time to express yourself and quit your job! Leaving a bad relationship is a healthy way to redefine who you really are.

> "AS A YOUNG CHILD, I WOULD LOCK MYSELF IN MY BATHROOM FOR HOURS, MAKING FACIAL EXPRESSIONS IN MY MIRROR."
>
> - Jim Carrey

79

Put A Star By The Emoji That Best Expresses Who You Are.

Expressing yourself should be easy and not complex. The divinity of creativity in your soul flows from a simple source. If it is too hard or complicated, don't do it. Wait until you feel the flow.

If you fail to express yourself, you will become emotionally constipated. Your passions are spiritual energies that must flow from inside of you. If energy, that needs to be expressed gets backed up, it will fester and swell. Frustration is a symptom of pinned up unexpressed energy. Feelings of sluggishness are signs of a stopped up emotional outlet. You need a spiritual plumber to unclog your energy pipes. Finding your outlet for expression is like using spiritual draino. What feelings are bottled up inside of you right now?

Let it go... scream... shout... go for a run. Do something to jumpstart the energy of your expression. Begin that business that you have been dreaming about. Start the hobby that you have been thinking about. Take cooking lessons. Learn how to play the guitar. Join a yoga class. Expression expands your joy.

Take a deep breath. Breathe out self doubt. Breathe in creativity. Breathe out the fear of failure. Breathe in imagination. When your lungs are clear of negative energy, you will begin to breathe out the true expressions of who you are.

Discover your real value?

Nothing has any value whatsoever, within itself. The **value is in the eye of the beholder.**

Example #1: A normal baseball bat is 34" long, made of wood and is worth about $10 on EBay. Another identical baseball bat is worth $100,000.00 on EBay. Why? Because it belonged to Babe Ruth! Same type bat... different value.

Example #2: An average handkerchief that is used to wipe sweat is worth nothing on EBay. A similar handkerchief wiped Elvis' brow and sold for over 200 thousand on Ebay.

So what's the point? The bats and the handkerchiefs were nearly the same. The only difference is their perceived value. Do you feel worthless or do you feel valuable? The only person that can answer that is you.

Low self esteem is a disease of the mind. Like a cold virus, you can catch it unaware. For example, someone made a mean comment about your weight. That is where your body issues began and you did not even realize it. Somebody hurts your feelings, puts you down, or makes fun of you... and you are exposed to the disease of low self esteem. The thought bug of insecurity planted itself in your mind. Self doubt has been festering inside of your brain since then. Self degrading thoughts left uncontrolled, breed and spread just like an epidemic. Insecurity left unchecked, can grow into a inferiority complex. Even shyness & timidity can be traced back to an exposure to a contagious germ of low self worth.

So what is the cure? The good news is that the mind disease is not fatal. There is a solution! But you will need to detox your mind. An effective detox of the colon flushes out disgusting toxins and impurities from the intestines. Detoxing the brain flushes out nasty thoughts of self pity and highly contagious concepts of self doubt.

A detox is only effective if it is followed by a change of life style. Going back to a junk food diet will only clog the colon once again. In the same way, after you remove the infestation of rotten thoughts from your mind, you must determine to block negative thinking from returning. Daily mental vitamins of positive affirmations will build your confidence and actually boost your immune system.

Look in the mirror and smile at yourself. Forgive the bullies whose comments and actions infected your personality with the plague of low self esteem. Determine to never let a comment or a circumstance affect your self worth. Don't allow a broken relationship or a job loss to produce thoughts that will clog your mind again. Let go of the concept that your self worth fluctuates with your bank account. Never value yourself with other peoples approval or rejection. Your real worth originates from discovering the presence of the divine inside of you. Your value grows in time, as you become aware of the power of the universe flowing through you.

The Baseball Bat................... $100,000.00.
The Handkerchief............... $200,000.00.
The Real You.................................... Priceless.

"Who says you're not perfect, who says you're not worth it, who says you're not beautiful! Who says!" -Selena Gomez.

I Forgive: _____ For: _____

82

DO NOTHING

◀◀◀ *Choose to*

LOSE

Check Your Do Not Do List

- ☐ 1. Stay in your rut
- ☐ 2. Sleep walk through your daily routine
- ☐ 3. Rely on chance
- ☐ 4. Be pessimistic about the future.
- ☐ 5. Make excuses
- ☐ 6. Become lazy and lethargic
- ☐ 7. Use alcohol or drugs as a crutch
- ☐ 8. Be bored and unmotivated
- ☐ 9. Resist trying new things
- ☐ 10. Believe in bad luck
- ☐ 11. Feel sorry for yourself
- ☐ 12. Give up on dreams
- ☐ 13. Be a couch potato
- ☐ 14. Be obsessively shy or timid in public.
- ☐ 15. Be uncomfortable being unique
- ☐ 16. Have daily mood swings
- ☐ 17. Be overweight and out of shape
- ☐ 18. Be apathetic and irresponsible
- ☐ 19. Have low self confidence/self image
- ☐ 20. Possess no self discipline

Choose to >>> WIN

Check Your To Do List

- [ ] 1. Learn something new every day
- [ ] 2. Write down a specific goal
- [ ] 3. Perform a random act of kindness
- [ ] 4. Develop a "can do" attitude
- [ ] 5. Practice meditation
- [ ] 6. Be accountable to someone
- [ ] 7. Exercise a little everyday
- [ ] 8. Dress for success
- [ ] 9. Have fun and relax
- [ ] 10. Celebrate the little things
- [ ] 11. Break bad habits
- [ ] 12. Go places to meet new people
- [ ] 13. Look for opportunities
- [ ] 14. Make a step by step plan
- [ ] 15. Visualize promotion and prosperity
- [ ] 16. Watch what you eat
- [ ] 17. Keep a journal of your journey
- [ ] 18. Expect good things to happen
- [ ] 19. Chart growth and progress
- [ ] 20. Smile! Smile! Smile!

DO SOMETHING

84

Don't Follow The Leader

☐ STEP 41

When I was a cheerleader, over 50 years ago, we measured success by if we won or lost the football game. Now, with thousands of life games behind me, no longer do I evaluate success by the score at the end of the game. Players who have the highest score are not necessarily the most successful.

The richest people are not always the happiest. Fame is not an accurate measurement of success. How many athletes, celebrities, and super models do you know who won the Oscar, or landed the contract, only to end up in rehab or failed relationships? Our culture worships rock idols and adores movie stars as role models to imitate.... BUT BE VERY CAREFUL, BEFORE YOU FOLLOW SOMEONE.

Be careful to notice where they are going and how they got there. Don't analyze their bank account to judge their success. Analyze their contentment with themselves.... their purpose in life... their joy... their love... their fruit. Real role models are few and far between. Remember every job, every marriage, everyday life has its challenges and rewards. Real lasting success is sustained not for just weeks, months, years, or decades, but for a LIFETIME.

The next step on your path is simple. Stop following others, and start leading yourself. Quit listening to the noise of the crowds, and start listening to the voice of your heart. There is a power in your heart that is greater than you. You cannot learn how to use it in school, or purchase it online. Real power can only be discovered by using it. Tap into your heart's power, and you will unleash the force of the universe in your life.

Success is a series of small disciplines, that lead to habits, that produce positive results. Be careful who you follow. Watch out who you look up to! Success is about making wise decisions instead of foolish decisions... no matter what the final score.

Success is a journey... Not a destination.

My Greatest Success:

My Greatest Failure:

"WHY DO WE CLOSE OUR EYES
when we pray, cry, kiss, or dream?
BECAUSE THE MOST BEAUTIFUL THINGS IN LIFE
ARE NOT SEEN, BUT FELT WITH THE HEART."
- Denzel Washington

Remember the

MAGIC

Do you remember how old you were when you stopped playing make believe? Do you remember when you stopped being a creator and instead became a victim? When did you stop being the cause and became the effect? Can you pin point the time when your dream became a nightmare?

As a child, pretending to be what you wanted to be was considered fun and normal. So when did you start not having fun and become abnormal. When you were young, you daydreamed of love and imagined happily ever after. Does growing up mean that you can't believe in the magic of your imagination and the miracles of your dreams anymore?

Just for a moment, forget everything that you have been taught by others and consider the truth that is in your own heart right now. Dare to believe that your true destiny here on earth is simple... you are here to give love and receive love. You are not here to move mountains or to change the world. You are not here to achieve fame and fortune. You are here for one reason... to discover that love is your true identity. Love is the path that will lead you back to magic and miracles. If you do not feel love on the inside, you will project lack and limitation on the outside.

The more that you give love, the more love you will attract. When you withhold love from yourself, you attract others into your life that will do the same thing. Every situation is an opportunity to embrace truth and reject illusions. Every thought of kindness can release your mind forward towards love. Every thought of anger can imprison your mind and push you backwards into the bondage of fear.

So your life has only the meaning that you have created it to have. All circumstances are neutral. Every thought that you think will add positive or negative energy to your situations. If you judge your situation as bad, you will experience the darkness. If you condemn and blame others, you will create black magic.

Judgement is the fruit of the tree of good and evil. Love is the fruit of the tree of life.

You have the ability to make anything mean whatever you want it to mean. You are only one thought away from experiencing magic. You have the creative power to turn a negative into a positive. You are only one thought away from your miracle. Dream with your eyes open. Remember your magic. Pray with your eyes close. Remember your miracle.

> "What you really fear **is inside of you.** You are afraid of **your own power.**"
> — Batman

My Destiny Here On Earth Is To: _____
_____

Find Your

Peace

Within

The

Problem

Is a problem a challenge or a stop sign? Everyone has problems. The difference is the way you look at them. Some people see problems as obstacles that causes them to quit. Other people see problems as challenges that provide a resistance that will make them better. Just like at the gym, the heavier the weight, the stronger the muscle. Everyone has a choice. You can run and hide from your problems or you can choose to face them head on. You can learn from the obstacles in your path or you can run away from them.

Alexander Graham Bell's wife had a challenge of being hard of hearing. This motivated him to create a hearing device, which evolved into the telephone. According to history books, during the same time frame, dozens of other inventors were working on communication devices but did not succeed. Many came close to a worthy hearing machine, but ultimately all failed, quit trying, or gave up. Only Bell had the motivation to keep going. Why? His motivation was to help his wife! When obstacles hinder you and when problems overwhelm you, there has to be a deeper motivation that inspires you.

In 1920, Clarence Saunders was fired as a young grocery store clerk because he could not retrieve the customer's orders fast enough. Instead of being angry at his boss or feeling sorry for himself, he faced his challenge of unemployment and created the first self-help grocery store, where the customers could retrieve their own groceries for themselves. This new concept was instantly successful and Piggly Wiggly became the first national grocery store chain.

All great inventions were created by people thinking of solutions to challenges. The car... the airplane... the microwave... all were inventions that solved problems. Trial and error... hits and misses... successes and failures... all are part of the process.

The solution to the problem always lies within the problem itself. For example, the antidote to a snake bite comes from the snake's poisonous venom. Vaccinations to prevent diseases are made from germs of those same diseases.

Face your problem and pull the solution from it. Allow the obstacle in your path to motivate you to create a way around it... over it... under it... or through it. Enjoy the challenge for what it is... a situation to make you smarter and stronger. Necessity is the mother of invention. Turn your problem into your passion. Allow your challenge to make you a champion.

What doesn't kill you makes you stronger.

"So you have problems? **Don't worry.** There is a support group for that. It's called everybody! They meet at the bar."
- Drew Carey

I Am A Better Person Because: _____

Change PERILS

Into PEARLS

Sometimes, like a freak of nature, a grain of sand from the ocean floor, seeps deep into an oyster's hard protective shell. It penetrates deep down into the soft oyster membrane inside. The sharp edges of the sand tear apart the delicate tissue and destroy it. When this rarity happens, the oyster's only defense against certain death is to secrete a sticky fluid from its immune system that will surround and cover the sand. The fluid forms a sticky ball, entombing the grain of sand in the center. The oyster is saved. The crisis is over. And the sticky ball eventually hardens into a beautiful pearl.

Without this phenomenon of nature, oysters are basically worthless. They sell for about $15 a dozen at your local Red Lobster. But an oyster with a rare pearl inside is much more valuable. It can be found at a jewelry store, displayed next to other precious jewels like diamonds and rubies.

How do you respond, when your own grain of sand gets under your skin? Do you, like the oyster, have a built in defense to counter life's potentially destructive intruders? For example, someone who you let deep into your heart, betrayed and hurt you. A particular circumstance that penetrated to your core is ripping you apart. Is something happening right now that is tearing you up? Just like the oyster, Mother Nature has provided your immune system with a healing balm that can cover, surround, and entomb your grain of sand.

Learn from how the oyster does it? Something signals the oyster to dance with the sand, instead of to battle against it. THERE IS NO STRUGGLE, THERE IS ONLY ACCEPTANCE... Situations in your life that you cannot change must be assimilated to become a part of who you are. Have you lost a loved one? Grief can destroy you! Situations in your life that you cannot change have the potential to make or break you. Respond with anger... no fluid secretion. Respond with bitterness... no secretion, more destruction. Respond with denial... no secretion, more devastation.

But remember, in life there is always another choice. Thank goodness, the universe gives us the example of the oyster. Respond with acceptance... suddenly their is a fluid secretion of a healing balm. Respond with contentment... more secretion flows. Respond with trust... the grain disappears under the sticky fluid. Respond with peace... the sticky ball begins to harden... Respond with joy.... moment by moment, as the phoenix rises out of the ashes, the brilliance of the pearl breaks forth!

Oysters who fail to respond correctly to the intrusion of the grain of sand are tossed aside at the fish market. But the rare oyster who endures the challenge and rises to the occasion.. remains. The oyster who creates a precious pearl out of the dance with the sand is worn and cherished by Queens, and hidden and stored in King's treasure chests.

The Biggest Challenge That I Face Right Now Is: _____

CHANGE YOUR THOUGHTS

The law of attraction is the law of magnetism. Like attracts like. You attract positive situations, if you have positive thoughts... You attract negative situations, if you have negative thoughts. Your thoughts are always drawing people, things and circumstances towards you. Look around yourself. What you are thinking, is what you're attracting.

My dog, Jack, attracts dirty socks like a magnet. His breath is the evidence of his thoughts of smelly feet. He's still a good boy. He's only a dog. What despicable things have you attracted to yourself? What evidence in your life right now, would witness to your thought patterns?

The law of attraction in any area begins as a mental game. Healthy people don't focus on sickness... Rich people don't dwell on poverty. Winners don't think about losing; therefore, they usually win. On the negative side... hypochondriacs stress out about illness and, therefore, are usually sick. Poor people constantly worry about money and, therefore, are usually broke. It's all in your mind! Whether you are on a golf course or a basketball court, your ability to win begins with your mental attitude towards winning.

How much time each day do your allow your mind to waste time worrying, struggling, complaining, blaming, fretting and fuming about your life? Negative thoughts create negative energy, that create negative results. Most importantly, you create a negative person. A negative person is usually filled with anger or fear.

CHANGE YOUR WORLD

> "WHATEVER YOU HOLD iN YOUR MiND on a consistent basis, is exactly what you will **EXPERIENCE** IN YOUR LiFE."
>
> -Tony Robbins

Negative energy affects your health, strength, emotions, and relationships. Start being aware of your thoughts, your emotions, and your mental attitude everyday. Be honest with yourself. Are you addicted to negativity? Are you a chronic worrier and constant complainer? Do you know someone who is? Remember, the squeaky wheels get the grease. But, if they keep squeaking, they are eventually replaced. Do you work or live with someone who is a squeaky wheel?

Negative energy drains the body of its life force. Negative people are usually depressed, lethargic, sickly, and generally in poor health. They usually try to regain energy by stealing other people's energy, kind of like an "energy vampire." They can literally suck the life out of their friends and family with their sharp, negative words. Their speech poisons the air like a bad odor in the room. They argue, scream, belittle, and complain to all the people around them, trying to regain lost energy.

Think of someone that you know who is a positive person. Do they have charisma? Do they draw people towards them? Do they seem to have animal magnetism? Now... think of someone you know who is a negative person. Do they bring everyone down just by opening their mouth? Do you feel drained and depleted just by being around them?

A Positive Person I know Is: _____

A Negative Person I know Is: _____

Find The Eye Of The Storm

The victims of the Holocaust were stripped of their identity, and given a tattooed ID number on their arm.

NO MORE NAMES, JUST A NUMBER.

They were removed from their countries and taken to prison camps.

NO MORE HOMES, JUST URINE SOAKED STRAW.

Their heads were shaved and their clothes were thrown away.

NO MORE BEAUTY, JUST RAW AND NAKED.

It didn't matter if they were doctors or lawyers before, now in the Nazi death camps, they all became slave laborers.

NO MORE CAREERS WITH SALARIES, JUST A PIECE OF BREAD AND A RATION OF SOUP.

Back then, how did prisoners remain so brave and so optimistic in a torture chamber abyss; while today, affluent men and women who seem to have everything, become despondent and depressed. The answer is the same. The value of life is in the eye of the beholder.

> "I believe that there is an inner power that makes winners and losers. The winners are the ones who listen to the truth of their hearts."
>
> -Rocky

So who survived the Holocaust nightmare and who did not? Strong young men died at the same rate, as fragile old women. Survival was not physical endurance but mental toughness. Only those people who could identify themselves as "survivors" outlived the torturous degradation. SURVIVORS were forced to channel their unbreakable identity label, since every other earthly label was unmasked and taken away. **Some could, some could not.**

How could emaciated bodies with no human dignity cling to life, while young healthy bodies today, find nothing to live for and spiral into drug and alcohol addiction. Neither affluence nor popularity keep people from creating their own abyss. How many times have we witnessed someone who has everything to live for, end up overdosing or committing suicide? The human state of mind is closely connected to hope and courage or the lack thereof. The body's physical immunity will correspond to the mind's mental condition. Mental decay produces physical decay.

This contrast is the proof that the mind is the key to your identity. People who have nothing can believe that they have something, even if all they have is hope. On the other side, people who have everything can convince themselves that they have nothing, not even hope. **Survive or suicide.** Discover the value of your own self. **Your very life may depend on it.**

My Biggest Accomplishment In Life Is:

_____

Make Friends With FAILURE

Failure is an event, not a person. I believe every failure is a blessing in disguise. I fail at something everyday. As humiliating as it is, I do not regard failure as a negative thing. I believe failure is nature's way of exposing weaknesses in your goal or plan, and thereby allowing you to make crucial course adjustments. Failure allows you to learn a vital life lesson, that will ultimately make you stronger and more successful.

Unfortunately, most people view failure as a good enough reason to quit!!! They then hurry off to a new adventure, which entertains them, until they again meet face to face with another failure. Thus, the never ending circle of chasing success, without ever realizing that failure is a vital part of the process. Failure is crucial to the attainment of your ultimate goal.

A baseball player learns to hit a home run by first striking out a thousand times. A musician learns to play on key, by first missing the note many times. The saying "*practice makes perfect*" is another way of saying, you have to fail many times before you succeed. Successful people are individuals who have the discipline to keep trying. Like the Energizer Bunny... they just keep going... and going... and going. They never quit... They never give up.

My own personal shyness as a child caused me to never raise my hand during class at school, even when I knew the answer. Later, that weakness escalated during my teen years to abnormal stage fright, which paralyzed my personality. After years of avoiding any type of spotlight, I finally overcame my fear of failure and actually entered the spotlight industry.

My fear of rejection has evolved & developed into a strong personality of steel. Everyday I still face criticism, but it no longer terrifies me. It actually now strengthens my character. I still fall on my face in front of others, which used to horrify me, but now I have learned how to smile at fear. I now know that fear is a part of life. It will always be a part of my personality. I understand that fear is only my shadow, it is not the real me. So If I am on stage, my shadow is behind me. If I am in a car, my shadow rides in the backseat. The fear of failure is no longer my excuse.

> "It's fine to celebrate success but it is more important to heed the lessons of failure." -Bill Gates

Failure

is like a
glass of water...
you can see it

half empty

or

half full.

My Most Embarrassing Moment Was:

_____

Be

The Best Of Both Worlds

On the horizon, the sky and the land, the heaven and earth, meet together as one. Two separate forms of matter, dust and air, but joined together as one world. In the same way, your physical body (earth) must come together and join with your spiritual soul (heaven) to form a complete person. Someone who is all about the body, but ignores their spirit will become shallow and egotistical. At the same time, someone who focuses too much on the spirit, ends up like a guru sitting on a mountain, missing out on real life.

The Eastern hemisphere culture overly focuses on spiritual growth, while neglecting the physical pleasures... leaving most of the population homeless and starving.

The West, on the other hand, overly promotes materialism, while neglecting their spiritual growth... leaving most people hollow and empty on the inside.

The East and the West must come together as the earth and the sky. Spiritual growth and material growth must both be promoted. Then and only then will there be balance and harmony in individuals and society.

Thankfully, today the two cultures are beginning to blend. Zen and Yoga are now accepted as normal activities in the West, while scientific endeavors such as housing projects and clean water research are no longer considered taboo in the East.

In like manner, individuals must learn how to blend their mind and their body.

When the part of you that is visible on the outside becomes conscious of the part of you that is invisible on the inside, you have discovered your whole self. The YOU on the outside joins with the YOU on the inside in the same way the sky meets the land at the horizon.

The fusion of mind and body is the key to life's mystery. The union of spirit and flesh is the secret of the ages. The combination of thought from your mind with the action from your body unleashes your hidden power. Like a dormant volcano that suddenly becomes active, something inside of you awakens and erupts. That something that was always missing is suddenly there. That missing piece of the puzzle that you have been searching for has finally made the picture complete. It is as if you have been searching for fire with a candle in your hand the whole time. It's like looking for your glasses everywhere, except on top of your head where they have been all along.

Yes, you can have the best of both worlds. Enjoy the technical advantages of the West, but also cultivate your mind, soul and spirit like the East. Personally, I am a little bit of a model, and a little bit of a monk. Yes, I am a weird combination... But I am proud to be me. Finish this sentence...

"The problem is **not the problem.** The problem is your **attitude about the problem.** "
-Captain Jack Sparrow,
(Pirates of the Caribbean)

I am a little bit of a _____
and a little bit of a _____.

Religion! Does that word make you uncomfortable? Does the mention of that topic make you cringe? Does the word "God" make you feel warm and cozy or does that word make you feel cold and awkward. How do you know God? Did someone tell you about him? Did you discover him for yourself? Is your connection to the force of the universe a thought in your mind or an emotion in your heart? Have you ever experienced an answer to a prayer? Do you believe in miracles?

There are hundreds of religions on the planet Earth. From Judaism to Catholicism... from Buddhist to Islam, they all are extremely different on the surface due to culture and race but basically similar at their core.

Personally, I grew up in a divided household. My mom was Baptist and my dad was Methodist. Looking back, it was like one was chocolate and the other vanilla. But basically, they were both *ice cream* .

What flavor is your religion? Is it bland and boring like vanilla? Or is it rocky road with a bunch of nuts?

Does your church have so many rules that you feel like a "Maze Runner" trying to find the right path to God?

Does your religion resemble the "Hunger Games" where God is like an old man on a throne being entertained by children who try to make it out of this world saved or lost? Does your preacher remind you of Denzel Washington in "Judgement Day?"

Behind the masks of dogma and the walls of doctrines, deep down, all religions contain the same basic theme... love and compassion... love for God, and compassion for those around you. Religion connects the human to the divine. Religion propels all people to be better. Sadly, many religions have wandered away from their roots and no longer resemble their spiritual origins.

Words like judgement and condemnation alienate us from God rather than drawing us closer to him. The term "holy war" is an oxymoron. Your spiritual label is the foundation to your social and personal labels. The fusion of your heart and mind is the bedrock of who you are.

It doesn't matter if you call communion with a higher power "meditation" or "prayer," they are both the language of the heart. You can bow your head or bend your knee. You can clasp your hands or close your eyes. You can pray in church or meditate on a mountain top. Both will connect you to the voice of your soul.

I Feel Close To God When I:

_____

"I have developed a new philosophy. Now, I only dread one day at a time."
-Charlie Brown

Exer

STEP 50

*T*hought is the invisible link between the soul and the body. **Thinking** is the communication between the visible and the invisible. **Prayer** is the magic between the finite and the infinite. **Imagination** is connection between the idea and the creation. Your mind can attract love and build success. The mind is developed by creating a desire and then imagining the results of that desire.

The mind is what sets man apart from the animal kingdom. The ability to solve a problem with his mind is what places man in dominion on this earth. A tiger lives by instinct only. A dog can learn to fetch a ball. Parrots can be taught to mimic sounds. But the animal kingdom does not possess a mind, which has the ability to imagine and the power to create.

The mind is your instrument to DISCOVER YOURSELF. How could an astronomer learn about the stars of the universe without a telescope? How could a scientist see microbes invisible to the human eye without a microscope? How could Mozart have created symphonies without his piano? The mind is your tool to solve your problems.

cise
your Mind

I Am Currently Learning: _____

The mind is your instrument to create solutions to situations. The mind is exercised with use. Just like lifting weights, the greater the weight, the stronger the muscle. The muscle of the mind is strengthened with challenges. When astronomers focus their mind on the sky, the stars reveal their secrets. The thoughts of dreamers gazing at the heavens have produced the creation of spaceships, which have transported man to walk on the moon. Engineers focused their minds on a solution to the energy crisis, and we now have electric cars that run without gas. Architects visualize buildings and bridges before they build them. Musicians hear melodies in their minds before they compose their songs.

So how do you exercise your mind? By focusing! By concentrating! What do you think about every day? White collar workers in business usually have a private office, where they can be still and silent to focus and to concentrate. In contrast, blue collar workers are out on the assembly line with noise or out in the store among the crowds. Blue collars usually do physical labor, while white collars do the mental labor. So what is the difference between the 2 jobs? The difference is **THE PAY-CHECK**!! Use your mind every day. Exercise your mental ability to solve problems. Concentrate on your goals and focus. Remember... The mind is a terrible thing to waste.

"**I believe** that people can move things with **their mind.**"

-Justin Timberlake

104

BELIEVE IT OR NOT!

True Story. Late one night, the foreman of a train went back to check all of his railroad cars one last time before he left work. All of his crew had left for the day, so he found himself alone by the tracks, as he continued his inspection. He noticed the refrigerated train car's door had been left open. He went inside to check it out, when by mistake, the door closed behind him, locking him inside of the freezer. He struggled to no avail to open the jammed door. He kicked. He screamed. He pushed... he panicked.... no one to hear his cry for help... no one to open the locked door.

He could only imagine his fate. How could he survive the night, trapped inside of an icebox? Surely, he would freeze to death before morning. Even though the large train car had plenty of oxygen for him to breathe, he was convinced that his body could not endure sub 0 temperatures.

The next day, when the crew came back to work, sadly, they found their boss's corpse lying in the refrigerated car. The door was bloody from the foreman's clawing and scratching at the handle. There was a good bye note found in his hand, saying farewell to his family, and describing in detail his fateful final night. Hour by hour, he documented his body giving in to the symptoms of frostbite and finally hypothermia. After writing that his feet were numb and his fingers were blue, the last entry was written at 5am. The note ended with a sad simple line, "This is it. I give up."

When the crew read the note, they were horrified. How could this have happened? Why was he dead? Yes, the door was locked, but there was still plenty of air to breathe. Therefore, he did not suffocate. The crew gasped at the content of the note because THE REFRIGERATED TRAIN CAR WAS NOT PLUGGED IN. The temperature inside the car was only 65 degrees. That temperature would not cause hypothermia or frostbite. It was actually the same temperature as outside of the train car.

So what happened? What caused his body to freeze in 65 degree weather? Unbelievable but true, his imagination led his body into trauma. His body created the symptoms of what his mind believed. If the foreman had only checked the temp gage in the car, he would not have panicked. He would have realized it was not even cold. He would have slept through the night easily and would have been rescued in the morning. Instead, his thoughts jumped to conclusions and deceived him.

The mind is a powerful force. It can play devastating tricks on you. Guard your mind. Be careful what you believe. Your thoughts are your gateway to your future.

"Be very sure that you're right. **Then go full steam ahead.**"
Davie Crockett (Killed at The Alamo)

My Biggest Mistake Was: _____

Don't Be Afraid Of the Dark

There is a light inside of all of us, that emits a radiance all around us. It manifests as the power of your smile and the sparkle in your eyes. Light is the love that you give and the joy that you feel. Light is the vibration that is everything that is good and true. But you must also understand that where there is light, there is also a shadow. Dark follows light, in the same way that night follows day. The darkness is connected to the light, as a part is connected to the whole.

If everything were light, there would be no depth or dimension to anything. In a spiritual sense, your light is also connected to your darkness. All of us are both good and evil. People who pretend to be perfect are only hypocrites, deceiving no one but themselves. Even in the greatest cathedrals of light, the home of the church, we all know that darkness lurked in the shadows. Horror stories of young people who were abused by church elders have unmasked the illusion of light pretending that there is no darkness.

It is now time. We can no longer be afraid of the dark. It is time to stop running from our shadows. Holding on to shame and guilt, will produce turmoil inside of you, and make you sick. Hiding your mistakes and covering up your darkness will surely suffocate you. Discovering yourself is to embrace all of yourself... the good, the bad, and the ugly.

There will always be a spark of light in the most vile sinner. No one is ever completely lost and beyond redemption. And there will also always be the potential for evil in the most holy of saints.

Hot and cold are both the same thing. They are just different degrees of temperature. Old and young are both measurements of time. The darkness and light inside of you are both measurements of who you are. The whole will never be complete if it denies part of itself.

A hot sunny day of light would not be complete without the shadow shade of a tree. And a dark black night would be incomplete without the stars to illuminate the void. Religions that shame and shun mistakes and deny the darkness usually end up as kool-aid drinking cults.

People who deny their darkness spend their lives trying to hide a part of who they are. Your darkness is your mirror image. Turn around and look at your shadow. Turn around and face yourself.

"Hope is the *only thing that is* stronger than fear."

- The Hunger Games

My Greatest Weakness Is: _____

DANCE
With The Darkness

Just like the marriage vows promise to love, for better and for worse... you must fall in love with yourself... both the light and the darkness.

In all of us, there is a DANCE of the union of light and darkness. Unfortunately, some people have changed that dance into a battle. They struggle within themselves, and create a mind that is tormented with guilt. To discover yourself, you must substitute the battle with a dance. The dance is easy to learn. Take one step forward and two steps backward. Then repeat.

Some days you will control your temper. And other days you will throw a hissy fit. You will win, you will lose. Yesterday you were good, so God owes you... today you were bad, so you owe God? No, it doesn't work that way. It is all part of the dance. C'est le vie.

It is what it is. Shadows cannot hurt you. They define who you are. We are all light. And we are all darkness. We are the shadow of the light. The day without the night is not complete. You without your shadow are not whole.

Yes, we all want to aim for the light. Yes, we all want to get better and better. Just remember on your journey, you will probably have to carry your shadow with you on your shoulders along the way. Quit trying to throw it away. You can never leave it behind. It needs you and you need it, to be complete.

ME AND MY SHADOW

Do you hear the music? Step onto the dance floor. You have saved the last dance for the best partner that you have ever had... the part of you that messed up... the part of you that was never good enough... Yep! Me and my shadow. It's a marriage made in heaven. The two have finally became one... for better or for worse.

My Hardest Temptation Is: _____

"FEAR IS NOT REAL. It is product of thoughts you create. Don't be mistaken danger is very real, but fear is a choice."
- Will Smith

Hold on... I AM coming.

When I was 24 years old, the doctors told me that I had a terminal disease. I am now 61 years old. That was 37 years ago. I didn't die... instead, I believed. Years later, when I was 35 years old, different doctors told me that I was going to die from a different illness. That was 26 years ago. I am still here... I believed.

So were the doctors wrong? No, I saw the sonogram for myself. But that did not matter, I still believed. Day in and day out, I believed. When death's symptoms surrounded me, I still believed. What I heard... what I saw... what I felt... did not matter. The only thing that mattered is that I believed.

I Need A Miracle To: _____

SO WHAT DID I BELIEVE?
WHAT DID I BELIEVE THAT SAVED MY LIFE!

1. I believed that I had a better reason for living than a reason for dying. Believe in the best, the best of anything always wins.

2. I believed that there was a light deep down inside of me that was greater than the darkness of the disease that was on the surface. Believe in the light. The darkness always disappears when the light is turned on.

3. Finally, I believed that the power of the universe breathed inside of me. So I took a breath. I am still here, I am still breathing. Believe in the power... Breathe in the power... Behold the power... Become the power.

> "There is no good news.
> There is no bad news.
> There is only news."
> -Kung Fu Panda Movie

BELIEVE IN THE POWER...
BREATHE IN THE POWER...
BEHOLD THE POWER...
BECOME THE POWER...

112

TRAIN YOUR BRAIN

☐ STEP 55

Thoughts create emotions and emotions create vibrational energy. Vibrational energy is the power of the universe that creates matter. In the beginning God said, "Let there be light." Science is only beginning to comprehend the amount of energy that was released during the Big Bang, when the words of creation were spoken. You too, can use the thought vibrations of your mind to create your own world. Your brain has the ability to desire love and to create a soul mate.

As children of the universe, we, too, have the ability to release tremendous energy with our emotions. Similar to the vibration of musical chords, a positive emotion strikes a harmonious chord, while a negative emotion produces a sour note. For example, the feeling of joy would create a sweet sound. The feeling of anger would create a horrible noise. The release of emotions, also releases vital energy from the body. Be careful where you spend your energy!

If you lose your temper, you waste precious energy.

If you are worried and stressed out, you could end up emotionally bankrupt.

Long term negative emotions lead to nervous breakdowns. Positive emotions replenish and restore the body's energy. Joy, happiness, and optimism energize the body, in the way that a charger energizes a cell phone. Simply by replacing negative thoughts with positive thoughts, you can plug back into the universal power supply and fill up your emotional tank. Connecting to the universe for refueling everyday will keep you from running out of emotional gas and from avoiding mental burn out.

Learning to control positive and negative thinking must become a daily discipline. Moment by moment, try to be aware of your feelings. When you feel yourself becoming angry, do you know how to keep yourself from losing control? When you feel down and depressed, do you know how to pick yourself back up? People who cannot control their emotions are diagnosed as bipolar. The brain has to be exercised just like a muscle. No physical exercise produces a weak body and no mental exercise produces a weak mind. Don't be a fat head. Learn to think lean. Train your brain.

Emancipate yourself from mental slavery. No one but ourselves can free our minds.
- Bob Marley

113

I Have To Learn To Control My:

114

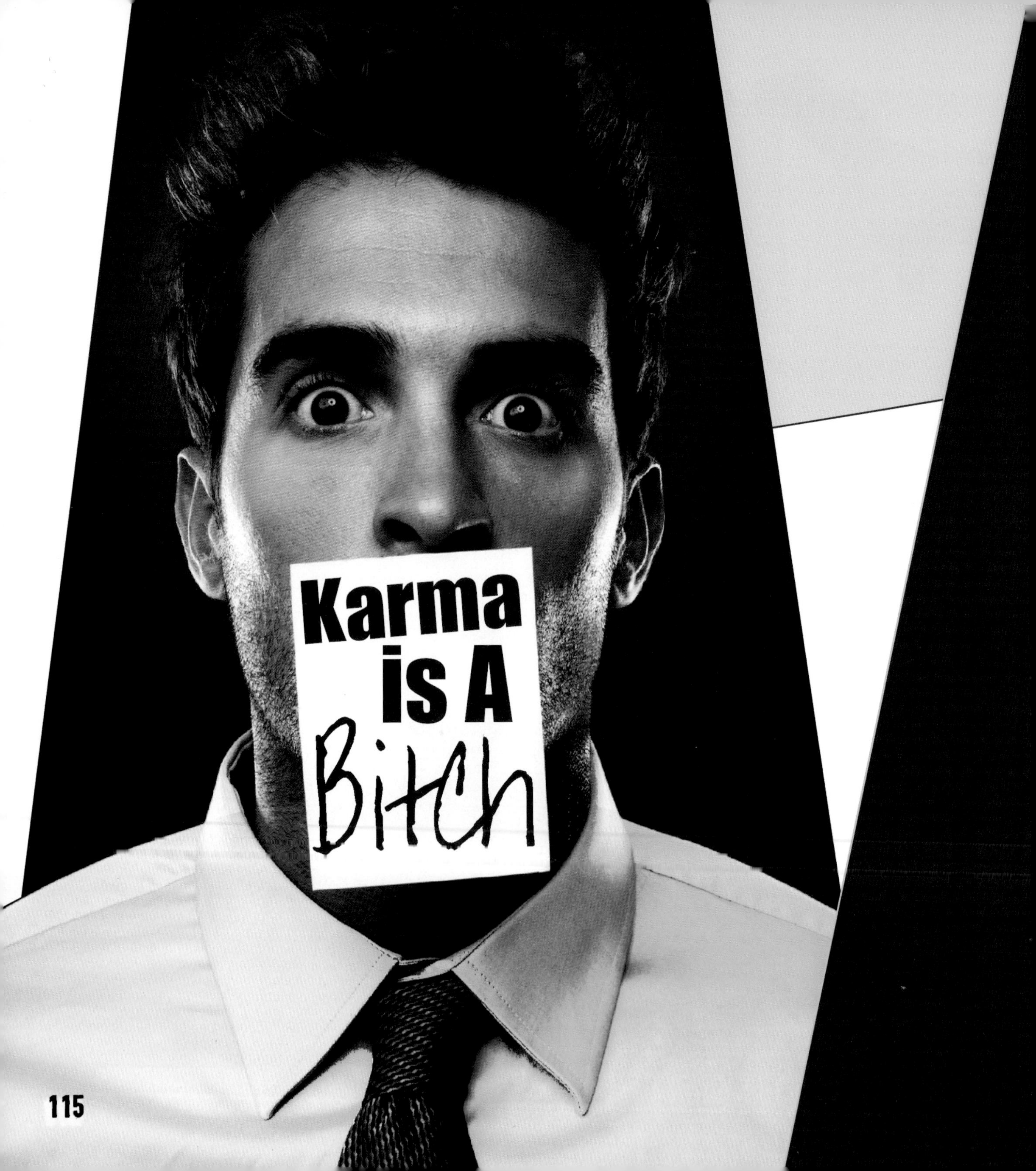
Karma
is A
Bitch

Correct Your Karma

The greatest power that we have as human beings is the capacity to choose to express who we are. Every moment of everyday gives us opportunities to use this power in our words and actions, while declaring and defining our personality and our character.

By simply expressing kindness in a situation, we become a kind person. To demonstrate courage is to become a brave person. In the same way, an act of dishonesty leads you to become a dishonest person. To blow up in a fit of anger molds you unconsciously into a mean person.

Before there is an action, there is first a thought. For example, before a murderer kills someone, he first must have had thoughts of hatred. Before a thief steals, they entertain thoughts of envy, greed, and lack.

We all have the power inside of us to create who we will be, moment by moment... day by day... by thinking, daydreaming, meditating, and praying; who we want to be. Everyone daydreams, meditates, and prays; whether they realize it or not.

Most people don't realize, that you automatically become addicted to what you think about. People who meditate and dream about sex, usually become addicted to pornography or abnormal sexual behavior. People who allow themselves to worry, usually become manic depressants or hypochondriacs. On the other hand, individuals who know how to guard their mind and discipline their thought life, usually become positive people with successful results.

The SECRET to making a thought become reality is *repetition of thought.* Everyday you will be tempted to be mad, angry or hurt. You must learn to recognize thoughts of jealousy, pride and hatred. You must learn how to breathe deeply and erase those negative thoughts from your mind. You must then replace them with healthy, positive thoughts. Five minutes of anger, can seep poisonous toxins into your body. Ulcers, strokes, and high blood pressure are all the results of a stressed body... and a stressed body is the result of stressed thinking. Unfortunately, karma is a bitch.

My Greatest Blessing Is: _____

"The word impossible is an opinion... not a fact.
It is just a big word used by small men, who would rather live in the world they've been given, **instead of exploring their power to change it."**
- David Beckham

Give Your Mind
A Make-over

Use this chart to help you understand the power that the mind possesses over the body. When your thoughts change, your physical biochemistry changes as well. Science has proven that mental healing has actually reversed physical disease. Quantum physics has documented the DNA in cells evolving from changes in brain waves. To develop a new mind set is to be born again. To put away your old way of thinking is to start completely over. You don't have to wait until January to make a new year's resolution. You can start today. You can think new thoughts right now. You will be amazed at what you can accomplish. Does your mind need a makeover or a takeover?

"I will not let anyone **walk through my mind** with their dirty feet."

-Mahatma Gandhi

Connect The Mind Thoughts... With The Body's Reactions.

THE MIND

A. Thinks Sadness
B. Thinks Anger
C. Thinks Laughter
D. Thinks Nervous
E. Think Romance
F. Think Fatigue
G. Thinks Fear
H. Thinks Stress
I. Think Anxiety
J. Thinks Desire For Food
K. Thinks Extreme Horror
L. Thinks Embarrassment

THE BODY

1. Butterflies In Stomach
2. Blood Pressure Elevate
3. Face Flushes Redness
4. Glands Produce Saliva
5. Belly Muscles Shake
6. Sex Organs Aroused
7. Lungs Induce Yawning
8. Stomach Acids Causing Nausea
9. Glands Produce Tears
10. Fainting And Unconsciousness
11. Veins Pop Out In Neck
12. Goose Bumps Appear On Skin

ANSWERS: A9, B11, C5, D1, E6, F7, G12, H2, I8, J4, K10, L3

118

Look in the

Mirror, mirror on the wall.... who's the fairest of them all? Can you genuinely say... I am? The secret to looking in the mirror and being completely content with who you see is simple. Look yourself right in the eye and begin to feel gratitude for everything you see in your reflection... your size, your shape, your color. Look deeper into your own eyes and smile at the person you see. Smile at who you are, where you are... what you are. Be patient. It takes time. *You might even have to fake it til you make it.*

The secret to smiling at yourself is to spend more time counting your blessings than counting your problems. Focus on what you have rather than on what you do not have.

Those who are grateful for what they have seem to get more and more. Whereas, those who murmur and complain about what they don't have seem to continue to spiral down and lose even more.

Ungratefulness is the root of bitterness, jealousy, envy and depression. These emotions create a face that is not "fair" to look at. **You can begin to actually alter your appearance by changing your thoughts.** Frowns on your face create lines and wrinkles that witness to years of negative emotions.

Your thoughts shape your face and give it its unique expression. Your thoughts and your moods project your overall appearance. A self confident mind will create a self confident walk. Positive thinking will cause you to hold your head high and hold your shoulders back. A weak mind produces stooped shoulders with a defeated countenance.

The shape of your body will reflect the shape of your mind.

People who think young, look young. A smile is a face lift. Happy thoughts project a cheerful countenance, in the same way that an irritable outlook projects a sour scowl.

Practice gratitude for your health, your family, your job, and watch your energy level rise. Then watch your health and relationships skyrocket. Gratitude harvests prosperity. **Gratitude changes your appearance from grim to fair.** Contentment softens a hardened expression.

Now look again in that mirror. What do you see? Now you should see the YOU that has everything, instead of the YOU that has nothing. Keep smiling at yourself in the mirror until the face you reflect smiles back at you. BEAUTY REALLY IS IN THE EYE OF THE BEHOLDER.

I Am Grateful For: _____

_____

MIRROR...

" *Alice,*
nothing is impossible,
unless you believe that
it is impossible."
- The Mad Hatter

Make A Vision Board of your

dream. Cut out pictures from magazines that personify your goals. Put the board on a wall that you look at everyday. A vision board can also be an index card that you carry in your wallet... or a post it note on your bathroom mirror. Be sure to include the "why" of your dream.

For Example:

If you are trying to lose twenty pounds before summer, you would put up a picture of the beach to remind you that you want to look good in your swimsuit. Do whatever it takes, to remind and motivate you to stay on track to meet your goal.

THE DESIRE OF MY HEART IS:
_____
_____
_____

I HAVE A PASSION TO:
_____
_____
_____

THE REASON FOR MY DESIRE
IS BECAUSE: _____
_____
_____

I WISH I COULD: _____

_____

_____

_____

ONE WORD TO DESCRIBE ME:

_____

MY SECRET DREAM IS: _____

_____

_____

_____

"If I can see it,
then I can do it.
If I just believe it, there's nothing to it.
I believe I can fly.
I believe I can touch the sky.
I think about it
every night and day.
Spread my wings and fly away."

- R. Kelly

THINK OUTSIDE THE BOX

□ STEP 60 Forgive Yourself... Start Over.

You screwed up? You really messed up this time. So what went wrong? You are stuck in a bad relationship and don't know what to do. You get up every morning miserable because you hate your job and don't want to go to work. You feel that somewhere in your past you went in the wrong direction. You took a left turn, when you should have taken a right turn. Now you feel like you are stuck in the mud and can't get out. You feel hopeless because you don't know what to do. You feel guilty because you know where you are is your own fault. You have no one to blame but yourself. You went ahead and married the guy, even though your friends warned you to stay away from him. You took the job even though your heart was not in it. You didn't listen to your own intuition. You ignored your gut feeling.

OK, take a breath. Let me introduce you to a dude named Jonah! He was told by God to stop what he was doing and go to a city called Nineveh. Jonah, being stubborn and pig-headed, basically told God to go jump in a lake. He not only ignored and disobeyed him, he actually flicked God off and went in the opposite direction. Like most of us, when we go against our own better judgement, Jonah ended up in the belly of a fish at the bottom of the sea.

How embarrassing. Real smart, Jonah. How humiliating. Look at yourself now. So what are you gonna do now, Big Boy? So who ya gonna call? How does that fish belly smell?

Well, if God was really the judgmental dictator like some churches portray, he would have just left Jonah in his own mess. Gosh, even Santa Claus would have put Jonah on his naughty list. Thank goodness, the God of the Universe does not work that way.

You probably know how the story ends. God caused the fish to spit Jonah out on dry land. Yay! Hooray! Happy ending! But wait a minute. Why did God save Jonah? Jonah did not deserve it. After all, he was the one that messed up. Doesn't God make a list and check it twice? Doesn't God know who's naughty or nice? Uh-oh... has the church confused God with Santa Claus?

Like Jonah, have you messed up and now find yourself sitting in your own hell that you created? Do you smell a little fishy? Don't be afraid. God knows where you are. He is actually there with you right now. Wait for him. He is there. No condemnation... only love... unconditional love. God doesn't send you to hell, he goes with you. **God is with us through good times and bad times. God is with us in heaven and in hell.** Jonah sinking to the bottom of the sea is a metaphor of sinking in life as low as you can go. God is by our side in our highs and our lows. He is with us on the mountain top and he is with us in the abyss.

SANTA CLAUS IS NOT REAL. Judgement does not exist. Separation from God is an illusion. There is no freakin list! The universe is not against you. God is good. GOD IS REAL! God is the universe... God is the ocean... God is the fish.

"Oh yes, the past can hurt. But you can either run from it, or learn from it." – The Lion King

"OOPS! I DID IT AGAIN!"

-Brittany Spears

I Am Sorry For: _____

MAKE YOUR GOAL
A DREAM
with a Deadline

A magnifying glass held still in one place over paper can create a fire. If it moves around aimlessly, nothing will happen. Focus all of your thought and actions in one direction. Quit skipping around from one thing to another. Just Concentrate.... and focus.

STEP 61

Someone once said that opportunity always knocks on every door. But by the time you unlock the chain, push back the bolt, turn 2 locks and shut off the burglar alarm, it is gone. A goal is a dream. A dream is a wish. A wish is a prayer. A prayer is a desire. A desire is a feeling. A feeling is an emotion. It all begins in your heart.

The heart sends the feeling to the mind. The mind transforms the wish into a goal. The universe then creates the answered prayer to your dream. Follow these steps, to build your life.

GOAL: _____

DEADLINE: _____

STEP 2: BE SPECIFIC

Don't just say, I want to make money. Write down a dollar amount as a goal. Don't say you want to lose weight. Write down the exact number of pounds, and the date that you intend to achieve your goal.

STEP 3: DIVIDE & CONQUER

We all have eaten an **entire cow**! How did we do it? One hamburger at a time. Every goal that you set should have daily, weekly and monthly goals. It's hard to imagine losing 60 lbs, but if you set a time limit of 6 months, it can be broken down to 10 lbs a month. Each month can be broken down into 2½ lbs a week. Losing sixty pounds then becomes possible..

"You should follow your own heart.
That is, unless your heart tells you to
eat a BURGER... In that case,
you should tell your heart that it must be confused."
-The Chick-Fil-A Cow

125

126

👍 Like Yourself

☐ STEP 62 *Shake Off Compliments Or Criticism*

Praise and criticism are the same thing. They are both measurements of other people's opinion about you. Neither one of them matters. Don't listen to praise. It will only puff you up and give you a *big head*. Criticism should be shaken off and dismissed. Ridicule and rejection are both forms of unhealthy criticism.

From mean tweets on the Internet, to bullied kids in middle school; everyone at one time or another has felt the sting of the judgement of other people. However, what most people do not realize is that praise is just as toxic and poisonous as criticism.

"Haters gonna hate. Shake it off, Shake it off!"

- Taylor Swift

Celebrities who are constantly stalked by adoring paparazzi become paranoid and withdrawn. Isn't it true that the more praise and popularity that a star gets, the more of a recluse they become? Many models and actors lose their identity as they are engulfed in a world of praise from other people.

Elvis Presley would come off of a stage where adoring fans were worshiping him, only to run away from all of the praise to begin his drug induced private world. He would then be given more drugs to wake him up and stimulate him to go out and face the praise of his fans the next night.

Everyone is born with a light side and a dark side. Elvis's God given talent was his light. His seduction to praise and criticism was his shadow. "The King of Rock & Roll" demonstrated a life of the struggle between good and evil... between flesh and spirit.... between mortal and divine.

Google the video of one of his last performances of the song "Unchained Melody", and witness the HEIGHT of fame and fortune... and the DEPTH of loneliness and depression. In this video, you will see his speech stutter to form a sentence and his hands fumble to remove a scarf. Then they suddenly transform magically into a voice with unprecedented clarity and hands of a master musician. One life.... two identities. Rest in peace, Elvis!

Sadly, Elvis was a role model for Michael Jackson, who followed his hero down the same path. Praise is just as deadly as criticism. Other people's opinions do not matter.

Your life is a reflection of who you believe that you are, not what other people believe or don't believe. Are you a *has been*, or a *never was*? It's never too late to be who you were born to be.

I Was Born To: _____

Redefine

☐ **STEP 63** *Who You Are*

ABUNDANCE: Unlimited positive thought

ATTRACTION: The drawing power of thought

ANGER: The leading cause of disease

BLISS: The state of inner balance and harmony

BREATH: The byproduct of human and divine integration

CAREER: Your opportunity to serve

CREATION: Thought becoming form

CHARACTER: The pathway to your destiny

COINCIDENCE: When the universe *winks* at you

COMPASSION: The ability to see yourself in another

DARKNESS: Shadows with no power

DESTINY: The purpose of your life

DREAM: Ideas connecting to the desire of the heart

"It's hard to beat a person, who never gives up!"

— Babe Ruth

DESIRE: What you seek that is also seeking you

DEATH: It is good. It is finished. The end of your journey

EVIL: Misuse of God's power

EMOTION: Energy in motion

EGO: The part of you that does not know that you are loved

ENDURANCE: The proof that you have not been defeated

FEAR: The belief in illusions

FAITH: Leap... And the net will appear

FAMILY: Your school mates for life

FLOW: Action with no strain or struggle

GOD: The invisible power which creates

HEAVEN: The knowledge of union with God

HAPPINESS: Contentment with yourself

HOME: Your school room for life

HEALTH: Perfect thought which manifests as perfect life

HELL: The belief of separation from God

IMAGINATION: To form a mental picture in your mind

INTELLIGENCE: The ability to make the best choices

JEALOUSY: The result of an inferiority complex

KNOWLEDGE: Learning the source of power

KARMA: The law of cause and effect

LOVE: The truth of the universe

LIGHT: Energy that illuminates God's creation

My Family Is: _____

_____

Reinvent

□ **DAY 64** *Yourself*

MAN: The image of *The Divine* in human form

MEDITATION: Dental floss for your mind

MONEY: Compensation for the value of your service

MANIFESTATION: The result of what you think

MASTERY: Successfully creating your dreams

PERSONALITY: The part of you that makes you unique

POVERTY: The belief in lack

PERSISTENCE: The visible evidence of your endurance

PEACE: Mental and emotional balance

POISE: Confidence under pressure

PRAYER: The voice of your heart

POWER: The result of the union of peace and strength

SATISFACTION: Knowing that you have done your best

RELIGION: Man's attempt to explain God

RICHES: Ideas of abundance

SIN: A lack of love.

SOUL MATE: Your best friend for life

"You have brains in your head. You have feet in your shoes. You can steer yourself any direction you choose. - Dr. Suess

SELF CONTROL: The personality and soul in agreement

STRESS: The pressure that creates diamonds and long life

SELF CONFIDENCE: No fear. Being equal to the task at hand

SOUL: The eternal divine spark that is inside every mortal human

SUCCESS: Doing the right thing, at the right time, in the right way

TRUTH: The witness of what is real

THINKING: The seeds of future actions

THINKING: The activity of the mind

UNCONSCIOUSNESS: A spiritual coma

UNIVERSE: The manifestation of the mind of God

VISUALIZATION: The ability to mentally picture your goals

VISION: The art of seeing things that are not visible to the eye

WISDOM: The ability to discern truth from illusion

WEALTH: Ideas of abundance

YOGA: Practicing the unity of mind and the body

I Have The Self Confidence To: _____

_____

132

Become PRICELESS

Everyone wants to grow old. Long life is the jewel of time. But, is there a secret to longevity? Can I take a pill or a vitamin to live longer? Is there really a secret fountain of youth? The secret to longevity is found in the same process that the universe makes a diamond... Simply, it begins with an ugly rock, a black coal; then surrounds it with pressure. The rock is compressed with stress. Then time does the transformation. That's it. That is the recipe.

Over time, we too, experience tremendous stress and pressure. So, how do you cope with pressure? Most rocks crumble under great weight and turn into gravel and sand. Most people crumble, under the daily grind of life's ups and downs. A black piece of coal can become a translucent diamond jewel, if it can only take the pressure.

I Feel Stress When: _____

> " When I turned 50 I reflected back on my life and realized that with age... comes wisdom."
> - Kermit The Frog

SO, WHAT ARE YOU BECOMING? Can you take the heat? Sometimes the pressure is so great, that all you can do is catch your breath. God is the breath of life. So breathe. How do you feel pressure? From relationships? From your appearance? From your job? Breathe... Breathe. Wait for it... Breathe deeply. Feel the pressure. It's ok. Feel the stress... Breathe.

Now, go out into the world and take control of your life. You have been called to conquer pressure. You have the destiny to become a priceless jewel of time.

Coal + Pressure + Time = Diamond

Youth + Pressure + Time = Long Life

We can live more abundantly every time we breathe, if we breathe with that intention. Breathe in confidence... exhale fear. Breathe in wisdom... exhale foolishness. When you finally discover that you can connect to the universe, you will begin to feel a surge of energy. When you use this energy to fuel your imagination, you will ignite a spark of inspiration. This inspiration will give you the courage to plan fearlessly and the wisdom to execute masterfully.

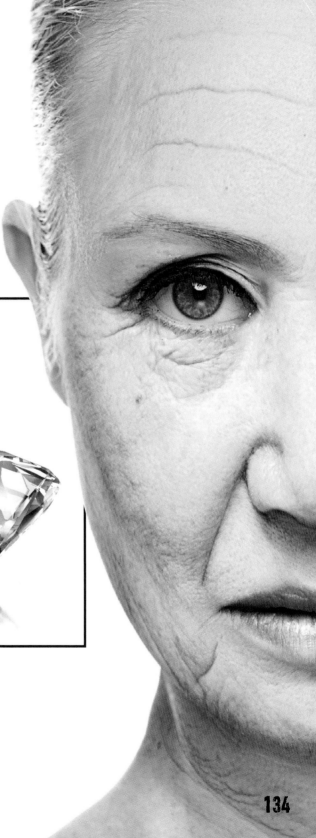

BE A STAR!

LIGHTS... CAMERA...

ACTION!

We are all given about 80 years here on this beautiful blue earth. That equals to about 29,000 days total in time. There is an old saying that the world is but a stage and men and women are all players in the theatre of life.

- So, if that is true, what part are you playing?
  _____

- What role have you been cast for in your own story?
  _____

- Are you the star? ☐ Yes? ☐No?
  Or are you only an *"extra"* performing in the background of someone else's story.

- How old are you currently? _____

- Are you now living in Act One or Act Two of your life story? _____

- Do you feel like you need to take an intermission about now and evaluate your performance?
  _____

- What are your critics saying about you?
  _____

- Do they give you a thumbs up or a thumbs down? _____

- Is your life an intriguing drama or a hilarious comedy? _____

- Is your story interesting and inspiring or boring with no plot? _____

- Most importantly, have you written a script for your autobiography here on earth or are you ad-libbing as you go along? _____

- Most actors prefer a well written, well rehearsed script instead of an improv performance. Just like life, making it up as you go can be frightening and unpredictable.

- Who is the director? _____

- Who calls the shots? _____
- Who is the author of your life story?
  _____
- Who wrote the script? _____

The answer to all of the above questions is... YOU ARE! You are the writer, the producer, the director, and absolutely the **star** your own life. So take control. Get ready. Get set. LIGHTS, CAMERA, ACTION!

"**Never bend** your head down. **Hold it high. Look the world straight in the eye.**" -Helen Keller

STEP 67

Leap!
And The Net Will Appear.

Dark clouds are on the horizon, the winds are getting stronger. There are sounds of distant thunder. But wait, this is a different type storm. This is not a rain storm. This is a category 5 "fear hurricane." This is a panic attack that comes over you like a destructive tsunami.

Billboards and TV commercials bombard us with advertising for the latest medicines to defend against the many plagues and diseases of today. Terrorists and lunatics lurk among the shadows, ready to pounce and ambush us anywhere, at any time. There are earthquakes and tornados... sink holes and wild fires... law suits and mean tweets... betrayals and backstabbings. Make it stop! Help! H-E-L-P!

Where are the life boats? Is there a life jacket that I can put on, just in case? Never mind. Rain coats will not protect us from aids. Umbrellas will not stop an assassin's bullet. The flood gates are broken and the tides are rising. People are being swept away all around us. Can't Siri give us directions to a safe haven? Surely Google has the answer! Where do we run? Where do we hide? No one can answer those questions but you.

My Last Panic Attack Was About:

Take a breath... Take a deep breath. There is a place of refuge. It is called the eye of the storm. It is located right in the middle of where you are. So how do you find it? The answer is simple but profound. You must believe that it is there. You must look for the eye of the storm. How do you get there? The path is in front of you. But you have to close your eyes to see it. Leap with trust, and the net will appear. Step into the waters with faith and they will part before you. Noah built an ark. He took the leap.

The blueprint for your own life boat is written in your heart. You can't learn how to build it in school. The instructions are a mystery. You can't buy one on the Internet. You already possess it. Neither the Republicans nor the Democrats know how to build one. Beware of their boats. Remember, the Titanic also claimed to be unsinkable.

God is the Alfa and the Omega. God is also the MIDDLE, which is located in the center of who you are. You possess the eye of the storm.

The power of the storm
that surrounds you is the same power that breathes inside of you.

Do not be afraid. Do not panic. Discover you... take the leap... The net will appear.

My confidence **comes from knowing** that there is a force, **a power greater than myself,** **that I am a part of,** *that is also a part of me.*
-Oprah

Create Your Own *Fairytale...*

Your *Once upon a time...* IS NOW!

Whether actors play a prince in a movie, or a doctor in a television show; at the end of the day, they return to being themselves. Balancing make believe and reality is a skill that must be mastered.

Arnold Schwarzenegger is an example of a mega movie star who lost his way, trying to balance being a super hero on film and being a regular guy as a husband and dad in real life. For several years, Brittany Spears looked like a deer with her eyes caught in headlights, as she was blinded by the flashes of the paparazzi. We all watched her emotional meltdown, as she shaved her head, and got carried away from her mansion on a stretcher. She, too, learned the hard way, that you must balance the make believe world of performing on stage, with the real life world of being an ordinary person. Sadly, Robin Williams and Whitney Houston paid the ultimate price with their own lives, not realizing that superstars have to play by the same rules as everybody else. It doesn't matter if you are a vocal or comedy legend, or a homeless bum who over-doses, a lack of self control and inner peace can be fatal.

So how do you find "happily ever after?" Your life is your own fairy tale. This world is an enchanted kingdom of dreams and wishes, hopes and prayers. The journey to discovering yourself will encounter heroes and villains. Sometimes you will laugh, and sometimes you will cry. There will be special effects that are actually only optical illusions. There will be applause, and there will also be boos. There will be praise from some people, and there will be rejection from others.

Wake up and be real. Focus on enjoying your journey every day. Take time everyday to be still and silent. Wait until you feel the magic inside you. It beats in your heart. It flows thru your veins.

Now write down your dream. Do you want to be a rock star touring the world, singing to sold out concerts? Start living your dream by singing anywhere... anytime! Remember, all professional baseball players start in Little League. Make your goals and desires very specific. Put your vision into words, then read it back to yourself out loud. This is your script. This is the first day of the rest of your life. Your story begins...... *Once upon a time...*

"NO MATTER HOW YOUR HEART IS GRIEVING, *If you keep on believing,* THE DREAM that you wish *will come true."*
– Cinderella